CULTURE SMART!
MALAWI

Kondwani Bell Munthali

·K·U·P·E·R·A·R·D·

ISBN 978 1 85733 878 2

British Library Cataloguing in Publication Data
A CIP catalogue entry for this book is available from the British Library

First published in Great Britain
by Kuperard, an imprint of Bravo Ltd
59 Hutton Grove, London N12 8DS
Tel: +44 (0) 20 8446 2440 Fax: +44 (0) 20 8446 2441
www.culturesmart.co.uk
Inquiries: sales@kuperard.co.uk

Series Editor Geoffrey Chesler
Design Bobby Birchall

Printed in India

Cover image: *Fishing boats on the beach at Cape Maclear at the southern end of Lake Malawi.* © Shutterstock.

About the Author

KONDWANI BELL MUNTHALI is an award-winning Malawian journalist. A graduate of the University of East Anglia, the University of London, and the University of Rwanda, he has served as a diplomat at the Malawi High Commission in London and a special assistant to the Vice President of Malawi, and is an ardent youth and public health advocate. At the age of sixteen he founded one of Malawi's pioneer youth organizations. He is a Niemen Fellow at Harvard University and is one of Malawi's key bloggers. Kondwani has worked for the Malawi Broadcasting Corporation and Nation Publications Limited, and has researched and worked on topics ranging from tobacco control in Africa to raising awareness of HIV/Aids, cancer, and child labor exploitation across the world.

The Culture Smart! series is continuing to expand. All Culture Smart! guides are available as e-books, and many as audio books. For latest titles visit

www.culturesmart.co.uk

The publishers would like to thank **CultureSmart!**Consulting for its help in researching and developing the concept for this series.

CultureSmart!Consulting creates tailor-made seminars and consultancy programs to meet a wide range of corporate, public-sector, and individual needs. Whether delivering courses on multicultural team building in the USA, preparing Chinese engineers for a posting in Europe, training call-center staff in India, or raising the awareness of police forces to the needs of diverse ethnic communities, it provides essential, practical, and powerful skills worldwide to an increasingly international workforce.

For details, visit www.culturesmartconsulting.com

CultureSmart!Consulting and **CultureSmart!** guides have both contributed to and featured regularly in the weekly travel program "Fast Track" on BBC World TV.

contents

contents

Map of Malawi

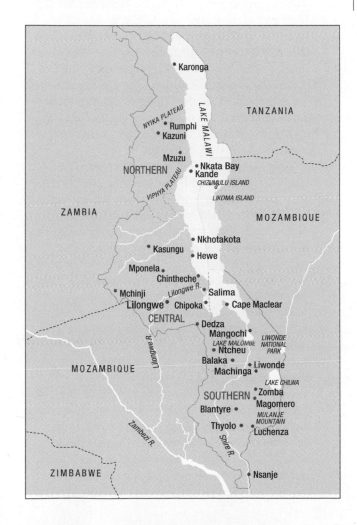

introduction

Variously nicknamed "the Warm Heart of Africa,"
"the Land of the Lake," and "the Land of Smiling
Faces," Malawi is renowned for the friendliness and
charm of its people and its dazzling lake. This small
country offers the full African experience. You can
land at the airport and within forty-five minutes start
out on a safari to see the "Big Five." You can enjoy
lunch and a walk in sprawling tea gardens, and later
sip a mojito on the beach as the sun sets over Lake
Malawi. All within a single day.

Lake Malawi, dubbed "the Lake of Stars" by
David Livingstone who first saw it in 1859, is an
unspoiled paradise, enclosed by mountains, with
long, sandy beaches. Part of the Great Rift Valley, it is
exceptionally deep and is home to many rare species
of fish, including brightly colored cichlids. The
country has nine national parks and wildlife reserves,
each distinct and unique, and mountains that include
the lofty Sapitwa Peak on Mulanje.

The people of Malawi are made up of a mosaic of
African cultures, ranging from indigenous hunter-
gathers to the incoming iron-working Bantu who left
their fourteenth-century rock paintings. Dress, dance,
masks, language, and traditional festivals all reflect
waves of migrating tribes—those fleeing Shaka Zulu's
reign of terror in the south, Swahili Arab slave traders
in the east, and Bantu from Central Africa. Other
cultural influences came through the slave trade
routes, contact with Portuguese and Indian traders,
and British missionaries who fought slavery and
bequeathed Victorian architecture and infrastructure.

Despite there being more than ten tribes, Malawi has remained uniquely peaceful, with many foreigners making it their home.

Malawians are, by and large, honest, quiet, conservative, good-humored, even-tempered, and inquisitive—sometimes to a fault. Their ready smiles, even in deep poverty, or at times when in trouble with the authorities, have been a source of debate, anger, and sometimes misinterpretation. Some have called them ignorant, some deeply superstitious. Their neighbors in Zambia and Zimbabwe considered them "sleepy" or "backward," and many have called Malawians their "wives"—only good for domestic work. In South Africa, where there is a huge migrant labor community, Malawians' honest character gives them leverage as adverts proclaim that "being a Malawian is an added advantage."

Contemporary Malawi is a mix of modernity and deeply traditional and religious values. It has a free media and a flourishing multiparty democracy. The traveler needs to observe the fine balance of the growing liberal urban culture, religious and conservative influences, mainly among the older and rural population, and the Malawian sociable impulse to share a word or two even with unknown people.

This book describes the forces that have shaped the Malawians' outlook and guides you through various situations so that you know what to expect. You will be received with warmth and great hospitality. Reciprocate with interest and respect, and your encounter will be deepened and enriched.

Key Facts

Official Name	Republic of Malawi	
Capital City	Lilongwe	Pop. 670,00 approx.
Main Towns and Cities	Blantyre, Zomba, Mzuzu, Kasungu, Luchenza, Karonga, Nkhatabay, Mangochi, Salima, Dedza, Mponela, Mchinji, Balaka	
Population	19.16 million	3% growth rate
Area	Total area: 45,560 sq. miles (118,484 sq. km), incl. 9,422 sq. miles (24,404 sq. km) of water surface, consisting mainly of Lake Malawi. Land area is 36,325 sq. miles (94,080 sq. km). About the size of the state of Pennsylvania or Portugal	
Terrain	A landlocked country located south of the Equator. Bordered to the north and northeast by Tanzania; to the east, south, and southwest by Mozambique, and to the west and northwest by Zambia. Much of the land surface is a large plateau. In the north are rugged highlands; in the south the landscape forms part of the Great African Rift Valley.	
Regions	Three administrative regions: Northern, Central, and Southern. The regions comprise 28 districts, each headed by a District Commissioner. The old colonial Eastern Region is retained for policing purposes.	
Climate	May–July: dry and cool; August–November: dry and hot; December–April: wet and warm	
GDP	US $6.4 billion (2017 estimate)	GDP per capita US $332.00 (2017 estimate)
Natural Resources	Limestone, uranium, coal, niobium, bauxite, phosphates, graphite, granite, black granite, aquamarine, tourmaline, rubies, sapphires, rare earths. There are oil and gas reserves in Lake Malawi.	

Currency	Malawi kwacha	US $1 = 725 kwacha (2018)
Languages	English and Chichewa are the official languages. Tumbuka is the dominant language in the northern region; Yao in eastern areas; Sena in the Lower Shire area.	Other major languages include Lambya, Lomwe, Mwanga, Ndali, Ngonde, Tonga.
Religion	75% Christian; 15% Muslim; 10% others. The biggest churches are Catholic; Church of Central Africa Presbyterian (CCAP); Anglican; and Seventh Day Adventist.	
Government	Multiparty democracy with more than 50 registered political parties	
Media	Malawi enjoys a free press and has two major dominant newspapers: *The Nation* and *The Daily Times*, both of which have weekend and Sunday issues	There are more than 20 TV stations, the major ones being MBC TV, Zodiak TV, and Times TV. There are more than 80 licensed radio stations.
Electricity	230 volts, 50 Hz	Three-pin plugs (British). Take adapters and transformers if required.
TV/Video	Satellite TV/ Pay TV	Digital multisystem video
Internet Domain	.mw	
Telephone	Malawi's country code is 265.	
Time Zone	GMT + 2 hours	

chapter one

LAND & PEOPLE

GEOGRAPHY

Malawi lies on East Africa's Great Rift Valley. This small, densely populated, landlocked country, roughly the size of Pennsylvania or Portugal, is bordered by Zambia to the northwest, Tanzania to the northeast, and Mozambique to the east, south, and west. Its lake, the third-largest in Africa, is part of the formation of great African lakes that include Lake Victoria.

Lake Malawi is the most beautiful feature of a beautiful country. Formerly known as Lake Nyasa, and still called Niassa in Mozambique, it makes up

one-fifth of Malawi's area; it is also known as the Calendar Lake, due to its 365-mile (587 km) length and 52-mile (84 km) width. Its water sources include the Songwe River, which comes from Tanzania in the north, and its major outlet is the Shire River, which flows from the southern end and joins the Zambezi River 250 miles (400 km) farther south in Mozambique.

The north–south Rift Valley is flanked by mountain ranges and high plateau areas. West of the valley, the land forms plateaus, generally between 2,953 and 3,937 ft (900 and 1,200 m) above sea level. In the north, the Nyika Plateau rises as high as 8,530 ft (2,600 m). The area to the west of the lake in northern and central Malawi has been designated by the World Wildlife Fund as part of the Central Zambezian miombo woodlands ecoregion.

South of the lake lie the Shire Highlands, which include the Zomba Plateau and Mulanje Massif. The Zomba Plateau occupies more than fifty square

miles (130 sq. km) and its highest peak is 6,847 feet (2,087 m) high. The plateau is one of the region's major tourist attractions. Activities offered include hiking, horseback riding, rock-climbing, fishing, and mountain biking. On a clear day, the city of Blantyre, Mulanje Mountain, Shire River, and Liwonde National Park can be seen from the plateau.

Mulanje Mountain, with its peak, Sapitwa—the highest in Southern Africa at 9,849 feet (3,002 m)— is dubbed the "Island in the Sky," rising in the middle of a beautiful landscape of tea plantations. It has natural rivers and forests including "Dziwe la Nkhalamba" ("old man's pond"), a natural dam that has impressive waterfalls and is good for swimming.

Malawi's strong belief in myths has not spared the mountain, believed to be the home of spirits. Some claim that on a visit to the mountain dam one may spot an elderly man sitting on a stone, fishing, before mysteriously disappearing.

The country has nine national parks and wildlife reserves, with Nyika National Park being the largest and highest plateau reserve with rare flora, birds, and animals. Kasungu National Park, located 165 miles north of the capital, Lilongwe, has suffered a depletion in wildlife stocks, due mainly to poaching. Liwonde National Park, with huge elephant and hippo populations, now has the "Big Five"—elephant, lion, leopard, rhino, and Cape buffalo—and in 2017 introduced cheetah. Another unique national park is the Lake Malawi National Park, which protects the diversity of tropical fish living in Lake Malawi—some of which are not found anywhere else on Earth—and yet another, Lengwe National Park in the Southern district of Chikwawa, is famed for its Nyala antelope.

The four wildlife reserves contain the Big Five and a variety of wildlife. They include the Majete and Mwabvi Game Reserves in the Southern Region, Nkhotakota Game Reserve in the Central Region, and Vwaza Marsh Game Reserves in the Northern Region.

Between July 2016 and August 2017, some 2,500 animals, including 500 elephants, were relocated from the Majete Wildlife Reserve and the Liwonde National Park to the Nkhotakota Wildlife Reserve. Prince Harry was the highest-profile facilitator of the animal translocation, which is aimed at boosting numbers of wildlife in the depleted reserves.

Wild flowers, birds, and waterfalls on many rivers, including the Manchewe Falls at Livingstonia in the north, Zoa in Thyolo on the Ruo River, and Kapichira and Nkula Falls on the Shire River, add to the landscape, which includes rubber and pine forests, natural boab, or baobab, trees, and vast plantations of tea, sugar, and other crops—all contributing their natural beauty to the mixed green scenery of Malawi.

CLIMATE

Malawi has a subtropical climate, which is relatively dry and strongly seasonal. The warm-wet season may stretch from October or November to April, during which 95 percent of the annual precipitation takes place. The precipitation comes mainly in December, January, February, and March, though the rains arrive slightly earlier and leave slightly later the farther north you go, and Malawi's higher areas generally receive more rainfall.

Annual average rainfall varies from 28.5 inches (725 mm) to 98 inches (2,500 mm) with Lilongwe having an average of 35.4 inches (900 mm), Blantyre 44.3 inches (1,127 mm), Mzuzu 50.7 inches (1,289 mm), and Zomba 56.4 inches (1,433 mm). Extreme conditions include the drought and flooding now attributed to climate change. The low-lying areas, such as the Lower Shire Valley and some localities in Salima and Karonga, are more vulnerable to floods than those in the highlands.

A cool, dry winter season is evident from May to July or later, with mean temperatures varying between about 62 and 81°F (17 and 27°C), and temperatures falling between 39 and 50°F (4 and 10°C). Frost may occur in isolated areas in June and July.

A hot, dry season lasts from August or September to October or November, with average temperatures varying between 77 and 99°F (25 and 37°C). Humidity ranges from 50 percent in the drier months of September and October to 87 percent in the wetter months of January and February.

Most of the rain fades by April and May, leaving a green landscape that is beginning to dry out. Especially in higher and more southerly locations, nighttime temperatures are starting to fall.

In June, July, and August, the days are still warm and clear, but the nights become much cooler, and some can be very cold, so that one needs to dress warmly on a night game drive, for example. This is the start of the so called "peak season" for Malawi, with cloudless days and increasing game sightings.

Into September and October, the temperatures climb once again, so parts of the country—especially the low-lying areas around the lake—get quite hot.

November is a variable month: it can be hot and dry, as in October, but it can also see the season's first downpours. Occasionally on successive days one can experience both weather patterns.

CITIES AND MAJOR TOWNS

Malawi has four cities, two municipalities, and several major towns and districts.

Lilongwe

Lilongwe, named after the river that cuts through the city, became the administrative capital in 1975, after it was moved from the old colonial capital of Zomba. The seat of government, Capital Hill, is situated in the Lilongwe Wildlife Nature Sanctuary, in the middle of the city, separating Lilongwe Old Town from the city center. The sanctuary rescues endangered animals and rehabilitates them. Lilongwe is also home to the Dzalanyama Forest Reserve.

The population of Lilongwe is estimated at 1.2 million, making it the largest city in Malawi. It contains Malawi's Parliament (opened in 2011), New State House, which is the president's official residence, and the mausoleum of Malawi's founding president and dictator, Hastings Kamuzu Banda.

Founded as a trading station, Lilongwe was formally recognized as a town in 1947. The city is separated into two. The Old Town, a remnant of the colonial trading post, boasts colorful fruit, vegetable, and curio markets, and old buildings such as the District Commissioners' offices, Old Town Hall, and Bottom Hospital. Creative traders have woven rope foot bridges across the river within Old Town, which people cross for a small fee.

The city center—a modern garden city with trees lining most of the roads and modern buildings—is where the seat of government, parliament, embassies, and international organizations are located.

While the city center is quiet by 6:00 p.m., save for its discothèques located around Presidential Way, the Old Town is lively all through the night. "Devil Street," named for its renowned pubs, market, and some nightly activities, is a twenty-four-hour locality where the general hubbub is punctuated by loud calls from vendors selling their wares during the day and rowdy assorted music from both established and makeshift beer halls. The drinks range from the traditional opaque Malawian beer, Chibuku, to whiskey. "Barbeque," which is roast meat that may be pork, beef, offal, cow's foot, or grilled chicken, is on offer throughout the night.

Other places to check in Lilongwe include the Bingu National Sports Stadium in Area 49, Kamuzu Dam, on the outskirts of the city, and private cultural centers such as Pamudzi, near Lilongwe University of Agriculture and Natural Resources, and Kumbwinja Ethnic Lodge, along the road toward the Zambian border.

Blantyre and Others

Blantyre is Malawi's oldest city and was the center of the colonial and missionary trading activities. It is named after the birthplace of David Livingstone near Glasgow, in Scotland. It has cold weather and is surrounded by mountains, which made it a favorite of the missionaries and early settlers. It is Malawi's commercial capital, and has major manufacturing plants, a shopping mall, and a vibrant nightlife.

Blantyre's older buildings include the Clock Tower, the church of St. Michael and All Angels, built around 1888, and the Mandala House, Malawi's first European building and trading house (see page 130).

Located 37.5 miles (60 km) from Blantyre is the colonial capital, Zomba City. It retains most of its colonial flavor, including the Governor General's residence and the old parliament buildings.

Zomba is a military and university town, home to Malawi's largest prison and the only mountain hotel— Ku Chawe Inn on Zomba Plateau. From Emperor's View, the highest point on the plateau, one can see Blantyre, the Phalombe Plain, the Shire River, and Lake Chilwa. Mulunguzi Dam has a scenic waterfall. The plateau also hosts the national botanic gardens, whose biodiversity makes it a must for eco-tourists. Birdwatchers will be especially thrilled, as the town and the mountain between them see five species of bulbul, five sunbirds, two twinspots, two unusual flycatchers, pygmy kingfishers, and the red-faced crimsonwing.

Mzuzu City in the north is a gateway to Nyika National Park, while other major towns of interest include Nkata Bay, which has sandy beaches and rubber plantations, Cape Maclear in Mangochi District, with its crystal-clear blue waters, Thyolo and Mulanje, with scenic tea plantation landscapes, and Karonga, which has a rich, ancient history.

Mua, a Catholic White Fathers' establishment in Dedza District, has a museum of the cultural history of Malawi, while the town of Balaka illustrates the development of Catholicism in the country. Likoma and Chizumulu Islands on Lake Malawi offer a mixture of Malawian, Tanzanian, and Mozambican cultures, and can be reached by ferry on the hundred-year-old MV *Illala* or the newly commissioned MV *Chilembwe*.

THE PEOPLE
This densely populated country is a mixture of Southern African heritage, Christian influence, Central African immigrants, and Swahili Arab slave

traders—a bouquet of cultures rarely found in a smaller land mass.

Malawi lies between three big African countries, namely Tanzania, Zambia, and Mozambique, and the joke is that during the partition of Africa at the Berlin Conference in 1884, after acquiring Zimbabwe and Zambia, the British were not sure about the remaining strip of land, and that it was only after a Scottish member of their delegation remembered David Livingstone that they insisted on having it as well.

This ill-conceived partition split several major indigenous tribal kingdoms, with the result that today the rule of their chiefs transcends the official borders. Malawi is unique in that most of its citizens pay homage to traditional kings outside their country.

The major tribe is the Chewa, who came from Congo area of Malambo in around 1480 and established a centralized kingdom, known as the Maravi Empire, at Mankhamba. Two powerful clans of the Chewa are the Phiris and the Bandas. The Chewa's current king, Kalonga Gawa Undi, is based at Mkaika in Eastern Zambia, where annually, during the last Saturday of August, Chewas from

Malawi, Mozambique, and Zambia pay homage to
him at the Kulamba Festival.

The Chewa, estimated to number more than
50 million across Southern Africa, are the dominant
tribe, and Malawi's first president, Hastings Kamuzu
Banda, who was a Chewa, declared their language,
Chichewa, the country's official language. Politically,
apart from Banda's regime, the Chewa have been
passive since the colonial period and have remained
largely loyal to Banda's Malawi Congress Party (MCP).

The second-largest tribe is the Ngoni, a variation of
the word Nguni, who make up two kingdoms, namely
the Mbelwa Kingdom of the Jele Ngonis in the north,
and the Gomani Kingdom of the Maseko Ngonis in
the center. The Maseko Ngoni originated in Swaziland,
while the Jele Ngoni originated in Zululand. Both fled
Shaka Zulu's reign of terror.

The two Ngoni tribes resisted British colonial
rule, with the Mbelwa Ngoni refusing to become
a protectorate and administering their affairs

independently until 1922, when the British convinced them to become a Native Authority; the Gomani are recorded to have been part of an early resistance, including the anti-First World War movement in 1914, in Malawi.

The tribes, however, have lost their distinct identity and militancy, with the Jele Ngonis largely adopting Tumbuka as their main language while their cousins, the Maseko Ngonis, now speak Chichewa as their language.

The third-largest tribe are the Yao, whose presence dominates the east and Lake Malawi's shores. They originated in northern Mozambique and were subsistence farmers until the coming of the Arab slave traders. There have been attempts to revive their culture, with little success, as politics has seen the crowning of different Yao paramount chiefs, different heritage organizations, and religious differences between Christian and Muslim Yao tribes.

Other major tribes include the Tumbuka (whose language dominates the north of Malawi), the Tonga and Ngonde in the north, and the Mang'anja, Lhomwe, and Sena in the south. However, tribal influences are minimally visible mainly because the majority speak the imposed Chichewa language. Most languages and dialects are slowly dying out, despite the introduction of news bulletins in other languages on the national radio.

The revival of the Lhomwe Cultural Festival, or Mlakho wa Lhomwe ("Meeting of the Lhomwes"), has seen other tribes vigorously revive their own identities; though a new pride in identity is growing, serious tribal conflicts are scarcely possible in a country where intermarriage between tribes is so common.

A BRIEF HISTORY

Traces of human activity in Malawi have been unearthed around Lake Malawi and in the Dedza Hills. Stone Age implements found in the region of the lake date from around fifty thousand years ago.

The earliest record of human habitation is the cave paintings at Mtakataka, which can be dated back as far as 1500 BCE. The paintings are the work of a diminutive people christened the Akafula, or Abathwa, by later arrivals. They were mainly hunters.

The Akafula were displaced by waves of migrating Bantu-speaking Maravi people from the Congo area, known today as the Chewa. In the late fifteenth century the Amaravi founded the Maravi Empire, which straddled the borders of Malawi, Zambia, and Mozambique. The king of the empire during its period of expansion was the Kalonga, whose

headquarters were at Mankhamba. The empire began to decline during the early eighteenth century due to fighting between its chiefs and slave traders.

The first contact between the people in present-day Malawi and Europeans was when Portuguese traders arrived in the sixteenth century to trade in gold, ivory, and iron. Later, when Zanzibar came under the influence of the Sultanate of Oman, the Arabs came to trade in slaves.

The Slave Trade

The slave trade was introduced into Malawi by Swahili Arab traders in the nineteenth century, following a great demand for ivory and slaves in the East African markets, namely Zanzibar, Kilwa, Mombasa, and Quelimane. The Swahili Arabs moved farther into the interior of Africa,  including Malawi, to obtain slaves and ivory.

One of the slave trading posts was Nkhotakota, on the shore of Lake Malawi, where a Swahili Arab slaver, Salim-bin Abdullah (known as Jumbe), set up his headquarters in the 1840s. About 20,000 slaves a year are said to have been shipped by Jumbe to the market in Kilwa, off the coast of modern-day Tanzania.

In 1861 the Scottish missionary and explorer Dr. David Livingstone visited Nkhotakota, where he witnessed the slave trade at its peak. He was horrified by the cruelty of the slavers, describing Jumbe's

fortified holding pen as "a place of bloodshed and lawlessness." In 1864 Livingstone visited Nkhotakota again and met Jumbe. He was able to secure a treaty between Jumbe and the chiefs of the Chewa, who were being raided for slaves, which put a stop to the trade and to hostilities between them. However, the treaty did not last long, as Jumbe simply continued his activities.

Another trading post was at Karonga, where the Swahili Arab Mlozi settled and terrorized the Ngonde people, seizing them and sending them as slaves to Zanzibar. He organized surprise raids as far as Chitipa and Zambia. However, he came into conflict with the African Lakes Company, formed by the Scottish businessmen and brothers John and Fredrick Moir in 1878. The Moir brothers had a mandate to supply the missions working in the country and provide a "legitimate" trade, as opposed to the slave trade, for the Africans. The African Lakes Company and Mlozi fought each other, but it was not until Sir Harry Johnston, the first British governor and an anti-slavery protagonist, sent soldiers in 1894 that Mlozi was defeated. He was tried by the Ngonde chiefs and hanged.

The Mangochi Yao chiefs, namely Mponda, Jalasi, and Makanjira, controlled a slave trade route that passed through the southern shores of Lake Malawi into Tete Province and the Zambezi Valley in Mozambique. These Yao chiefs terrorized the peaceful Nyanja, a branch of the Maravi people who lived in the Upper Shire and southern shores of Lake Malawi.

Yao chiefs controlled another slave trade route, which passed through the southern highlands: Nyezerera and Mkanda controlled the sub-route between Mulanje Mountain and Michesi Hill, in what is now Phalombe District; Chikumbu and Matipwiri controlled the sub-route through the southern part of Mulanje Mountain. They terrorized the Nyanja people in the Shire Highlands and the Mang'anja of the Lower Shire Valley.

It is important to understand the extent of the slave trade, which had a profound impact on Malawi's culture and tribal relations, and created long-running suspicions between Christians and Muslims until well after independence.

Britain declared Nyasaland a protectorate in 1891, with Sir Harry Johnstone becoming governor-general of the new protectorate. This marked the end of the slave trade. Most tribes that had been terrorized by the slave traders quickly accepted British protection and submitted to their rule without resistance.

Christianity

British missionaries introduced Christianity to the region in the nineteenth century. In 1859 David Livingstone arrived at Lake Malawi, which he called Lake Nyasa, a Yao word for "lake." Within two years of the "discovery" of Lake Nyasa, in 1861 Livingstone brought the Universities Mission to Central Africa (UMCA), under Bishop Frederick Mackenzie, to Magomero, in Chiradzulo District.

The Christian missionaries encountered resistance from the Yao people, who had settled in Magomero before 1860 and had embraced Islam. Bishop Mackenzie and Livingstone sided with the Mang'anja, who were non-Muslims. When war erupted between the Yao and the Mang'anja, Bishop Mackenzie and Livingstone supported the Mang'anja campaign to expel the Yao and burn their houses and fields. The involvement of Livingstone at Magomero in 1861 is not explicitly stated in the history textbooks of Malawi.

The arrival of the UMCA in Nyasaland was followed by other Christian Churches, namely the Dutch Reformed Church, the Free Church of Scotland, and eventually the Catholic Church in 1889. Religion has since then been a vital social and political influence on the people of Malawi.

The Colonial Period, 1891–1964

The Church's influence grew considerably, and for a few years agriculture, brought by white missionaries, including tea in the Shire Highlands and tobacco in the Central Region, saw locals settle for a quiet life.

A US-educated African Baptist pastor, the Reverend John Chilembwe, had founded the Providence Industrial Mission at Magomero, which preached the values of hard work, self-respect, and self-help. Over time, Chilembwe became increasingly critical of the exploitation of Africans by the white landowners, who were using a forced labor system called *thangata* (this, in pre-colonial times, had been a traditional form of freely given reciprocal help). He led a short uprising in January 1915, mainly protesting against the involvement of Africans in the First World War and the ill-treatment of African workers by white farmers. This led to the killing of a white farmer, William Livingstone, near Magomero. The colonial government quickly suppressed the uprising, and Chilembwe was killed as he fled toward Mozambique. Chilembwe is considered a hero today and is honored with a national holiday on January 15; his portrait is on Malawi's currency notes.

Political resistance against the colonial administration was largely uncoordinated. Native Associations were

first formed in 1912, and then in the 1920s and
'30s. Finally a formal political party, the Nyasaland
African Congress (NAC), was formed in 1943. In
October 1944, the Congress elected Levi Ziliro
Mumba as its first president. Another pioneer, James
Frederick Sangala, was elected to the executive
committee after being transferred from Blantyre to
Dedza by the colonial authorities. In January 1945,
Mumba died and was replaced by Charles Matinga.
The NAC was weak until its revival in 1950, when
James Chinyama was elected president, with Sangala
as his deputy. By this time the Congress was being
financially supported by Hastings Kamuzu Banda, a
Malawian doctor who was based in England.

Their thinking was that Nyasaland would evolve
into self-rule under the British protectorate, but
this hope was squashed when the Federation of
Rhodesia and Nyasaland—consisting of Southern
Rhodesia (now Zimbabwe), Nyasaland (Malawi),
and Northern Rhodesia (Zambia)—was declared on
August 1, 1953. In 1954 Sangala became president
of the NAC, which now campaigned vigorously for
greater African representation in the Nyasaland
Legislative Council, and in 1957 demanded an
African majority in the Council. The veteran
Sangala was persuaded to step down and hand over
to a more radical younger man, T. D. T. Banda (no
relation to Hastings), who, however, was soon forced
to resign under a cloud. In response to pleas from
the Congress leadership, Hastings Banda returned to
Nyasaland in 1958 and assumed the presidency
of the NAC.

Banda's speaking tours across the country stirred up unrest, and on March 3, 1959, a state of emergency was declared. The NAC was banned, and hundreds of Congress supporters, including Banda, were arrested and shipped off to jail in Gweru, in Southern Rhodesia, where Banda remained until 1960.

In 1959 Nyasaland's first lawyer, Orton Chirwa, formed the Malawi Congress Party (MCP) to replace the NAC, and passed on the leadership to Banda on his release. The MCP contested and won all legislative seats in elections held in 1961. Banda became prime minister in 1963. On July 6, 1964, Nyasaland became independent and adopted the name Malawi.

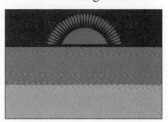

Hastings Kamuzu Banda, 1964–94

In August 1964, a month after independence, cabinet ministers disagreed with Banda on various policy fronts, including relations with the Eastern Bloc, as many wanted to follow the Non-Aligned Movement, and ministers wanted to curb his powers as he was becoming autocratic. Banda threatened to resign and mobilized the Youth League of his party to deal with what were now termed "dissidents." Many ministers resigned in solidarity with their colleagues, notably Henry Masauko Chipembere, who briefly took up arms to oust Banda.

Banda and his loyalists, who had inherted the colonial security apparatus, quickly quashed the rebellion, and in 1966, when he was sworn in as the first republican president, the MCP became the only party in Malawi. He arrested perceived opponents, banned the Jehovah's Witnesses, continued the colonial law of detention without trial, and introduced a forfeiture act to confiscate the properties of his political rivals.

In 1971 Banda was proclaimed President for Life. If, today, you see Malawians smartly dressed all the time, in ties even in intense heat, this is a hangover from Banda's thirty-one years of dictatorship, where he was only ever seen in public dressed in a three-piece suit, speaking only English in public—mainly in self-praise—and singing of uniting the Malawian tribes and bringing development. He kept himself aloof, a figure of mystery, so much so that people feared mentioning his name in public or even tearing a newspaper showing a picture of his face. Schoolchildren lined the streets to clap as he passed, and women and young girls composed praise songs that dominated the nation's only radio station.

More than 25,000 books, films, and newspapers were banned under the country's censorship act, as was television (though Banda had satellite television at his palace), and the Decency in Dress Act banned men from sporting dreadlocks or long hair, and women from wearing mini skirts and pants (see pages 56–59).

Banda is credited with enforcing discipline and peace, despite the reign of terror over which he presided. During the Cold War he was a favorite

of the West, which ignored his poor human rights record and open acceptance of apartheid South Africa, and poured money into his coffers.

Infrastructure improved; so too did Banda's pet economic empire, the Press Corporation, which almost collapsed in 1978 and could have brought the whole Malawi economy down with it. Banda effectively owned and controlled 30 percent of the economy through the corporation. A loan was obtained to restructure the corporation and it became a public trust.

The end of the Cold War and a campaign for human rights across the Western World hastened the end of Banda's rule. Global figures, from the UK's Margaret Thatcher and US Vice President Dan Quayle to Pope John Paul II and the Archbishop of Canterbury, all visited Banda between 1989 and 1991.

Kamuzu Mysteries

Banda, a lifelong bachelor, lived with his "official hostess," Cecilia Tamanda Kadzamira, whose title included "Mama," or mother, and was known as such by the whole country. Nobody has explained the close relationship between the two, and a Mr. Sangala, a CCAP minister who is alleged to have suggested that they exchange marriage vows, mysteriously disappeared.

Banda used to carry a flywhisk, which, in a society of deep beliefs and superstitions, was feared to contain powers to fend off political opponents. It was believed that he could hear or see everything in the country.

Nobody was allowed to mention Banda's first name, or that of Kadzamira. His official title ran as "His Excellency the Life President, Ngwazi Dr. H. Kamuzu Banda, Lion of Malawi, Destroyer of Federation of Rhodesia and Nyasaland, Farmer Number 1, Protector and Counsellor of all Women," among others, with party zealots calling him "The Messiah."

It was again the Church, which remains influential in Malawi, that ignited the internal calls for multiparty democracy when, in March 1991, the Catholic bishops released a Pastoral Letter openly rebuking Banda for his human rights record. Brief strikes ensued, bishops were threatened with death, and an Irish priest was deported. An exiled trade unionist, Chakufwa Chihana, defied Banda and landed in Malawi on April 6, 1991. He was arrested at the airport and later jailed until Banda's referendum.

Succumbing to the pressure, Banda called for a referendum on June 14, 1993, in which Malawians overwhelmingly voted for multiparty democracy. On May 17, 1994, almost thirty years since independence, Malawi ousted Banda and elected businessman and former MCP Secretary General Bakili Muluzi as President. Banda died three years later, on November 25, 1997.

PRESENT-DAY POLITICS

Today Malawi is a fully-fledged democracy, despite the fact that the president and the executive branch wield power that many feel is excessive. The bill of rights in the constitution is protected, and can be amended only through a referendum—a lesson well learned from Banda's era, when he simply enacted laws that suited his agenda. Since 1994, four presidents have been elected, namely Bakili Muluzi of the United Democratic Front (UDF), 1994–2004; Bingu wa Mutharika, first UDF, 2004–09, then the Democratic Progressive Party (DPP), 2009–12; Joyce Banda of the

People's Party, 2012–14; and Peter Mutharika of the DPP, elected in 2014.

The constitution limits the president to two terms, and attempts to change the constitution in 2002 were rejected. Malawians have suddenly become fearless defenders of their democracy. On July 20, 2011, massive demonstrations left twenty people dead after being shot by police in a protest against what were thought to be excesses by then president Bingu wa Mutharika.

Politics in Malawi is largely personalized, based on personal loyalties rather than political ideology, with the manifestos of all the major parties revolving around the core issues that affect the majority of poor voters—food security, education, health, and poverty alleviation.

Voting tends to be based on regional lines, with the Southern Region producing all the presidents since Banda's day, and the Central Region remaining closely aligned to the MCP. The Northern Region, whose population is small, and which has only thirty-one of the 193 parliamentary seats, is largely seen as power broker, though it has changed its voting at every election, voting for the Alliance for Democracy in 1994, the MCP in 1999, the Mgwirizano Coalition in 2004, the DPP in 2009, and the People's Party in 2014.

The elections are first-past-the-post: a plurality voting method in which the candidate with the most votes wins, as opposed to a system of proportional representation. This has seen presidents and members of parliament win with narrow majorities. Parliament has a high turnover rate, with more than 60 percent of its membership being dumped by voters at each election.

The local councils have been revitalized since the 2014 elections, adding excitement to the electoral and political scene—the mayors and chairpersons of local councils have to stand for election every two and half years and every year respectively, adding to the rivalry between the government and opposition parties.

For a people once mocked by their neighbors in Zambia and Zimbabwe as "wives" or "puppets," the Malawians have shown remarkable strength in collectively defending their democracy. They can afford to joke about the Zimbabweans' massive failure to remove President Robert Mugabe, who managed to surpass Banda's long reign.

GOVERNMENT

Malawi is a republic with a presidential system of government. The president is elected directly by the voters alongside a running mate for the position of vice president, who cannot subsequently be removed by the president. The president is the head of the Executive and can be elected even without commanding a

majority in parliament. He can appoint members of his cabinet from outside or inside parliament.

Parliament consists of the president and members of the National Assembly, which is independent of the Executive. Its core function is to provide checks and balances to the Executive. It passes the national budget and enacts legislation. Parliament has become the most followed political institution, as its debates are aired live, and usually the government is taken to task by the opposition. Parliament is headed by the speaker, who is elected by the members. The opposition has elected its own member as speaker after each election, mainly due to their numbers in parliament, save for 1999 and 2009.

The third branch is the Judiciary, which has a remarkable history of independence, even during the one-party regime. The courts have at times become the sole focus of Malawi politics, especially in election-related disputes or demands for recounts, protection of citizens against new laws, and protecting the rights of the citizenry. Malawi's legal system is both a common law and civil law system. The country's law school at Chancellor College has for years provided the only acceptable qualification to practice law in Malawi. Reforms, however, have introduced bar exams for holders of qualifying law degrees from outside Malawi to enable them to practice in the country.

The Electoral Process
Since 2014 the elections for president, members of parliament, and councilors have been held at the same

time, for terms of five years. The electoral process is a year-long affair and provides a carnival atmosphere for visitors as parties compete in dressing up supporters and putting up campaign posters and other materials on trees and along roads. The most competitive and popular rallies are the presidential campaigns. These are normally huge and well-designed festivals, complete with traditional dances, music, and speeches, that are unequalled by any other elections in Africa.

The process is expensive, with no guarantee for anybody to win, especially the parliamentary elections, where the numbers of independent, as opposed to party, candidates have been growing with each election. Since 1994, only one president has won two elections on the same party ticket, one has changed parties in two elections, and a sitting president has lost an election, making Malawi's elections most unpredictable, if mostly peaceful.

Despite cries, naturally mainly from the losers, of cheating at the polls, the Electoral Commission, which is chaired by a Supreme Court judge and with Commissioners from all the major parties represented in parliament, has striven to improve the credibility of elections, involving all the parties throughout the electoral process.

THE ECONOMY
Population
Malawi's population is estimated to have reached more than 18 million. It has one of the highest population densities in Southern Africa, and its high birth rate

makes it one of the most fertile countries on the continent. Early marriages—especially in the rural areas, where roughly 80 percent of the population live—and poverty have been identified as contributing to the large amount of free time that allows people to indulge in sexual activity. The deep religious and cultural norms in most villages can safely be assumed to be factors that encourage sexual activity at an early age. At puberty both girls and boys are taken for special counseling sessions, as part of the rites of passage initiation ceremonies, which include tuition on the ways to please a partner, and adolescents are encouraged to "test the equipment" after the initiation.

As in other cultures, for the poorest communities, finding a richer husband or marrying a daughter into a wealthier family can be a way out of poverty. A girl might have little say in the matter, though there are current initiatives and interventions to end the practice. Among urbanites and in educated communities most people limit the number of children they have, though teenage pregnancies have been a rising challenge in these groups.

The HIV/AIDS pandemic has complicated Malawi's demographic picture, with child-headed households and orphanages becoming more common as many parents succumb, often leaving vulnerable children, who may then be abused or trafficked.

Agriculture

Malawi is largely an agricultural country About 84 percent of people live in rural areas and are primarily engaged in subsistence farming on small farms, or

"smallholdings." Agriculture accounts for more than
one-third of GDP and 90 percent of exports.

Tobacco, tea, sugar, cotton, coffee, timber, and
dried legumes are the main export crops. Tobacco
alone is estimated to account for 60–70 percent of the
country's exports and takes up 4 percent of farmland.

Smallholder farmers contribute 75 percent of the
food consumed and cultivate some 20,463 sq. miles
(5.3 million hectares) of arable land. Maize, cassava,
sweet potatoes, rice, sorghum, groundnuts (peanuts),
and pulses (legumes) are important food crops. Most
of the land in Malawi is "customary," that is, it belongs
to families and is inherited, and laws were introduced
in 2016 to recognize this legally, adding value to poor
households' income status. The chiefs adjudicate
land matters.

The government-supported Green Belt initiative
aims to irrigate 3,861 sq. miles (1 million hectares)
of land to counter the effects of climate change,
to mechanize farming, and thus to increase the
opportunities for smallholder farmers.

Fish farming and agro-processing for exports are among key focus areas as Malawi enjoys preferential trading agreements with the European Union, the USA, China, and regional African markets.

Energy

Malawi's manufacturing sector has been directly affected by its limited sources of energy—its total generation capacity is around 356 megawatts. Only about 10 percent of Malawians have access to electricity. Liberalization of the sector, including the unbundling of the state-owned energy monopoly Electricity Supply Commission of Malawi, was completed on December 31, 2016. The sector is now open for investment: a 1,000-megawatt plant at Kammwamba, in the southern district of Balaka, is expected to be financed by China, and there are dozens of other small electricity generation projects starting up, enabling Malawi to become a center of manufacturing. Renewable and clean energy projects are among most recent investments.

Mining

Malawi is naturally endowed with mineral deposits of uranium, rare earth metals, alluvial gold, gold, limestone, coal, bauxite, gemstones, and niobium. A mineral map made by the British Geographical Society in 2008 indicates the extent of the potential of these high-value minerals. Uranium mining was started by the Australian firm Paladin, but put on hold as metal prices tumbled, and other large projects such as the mining of niobium in the Central Region are waiting for financing. Rare-earth exploration is at an advanced stage in Southern Malawi, and the company Mkango Resources, registered in Canada and floated on the London Stock Exchange, expects to start operations within the next five years. Despite the huge mining potential, lack of expertise and poor energy sources have delayed the full realization of the sector.

Oil and Gas

Oil was first discovered in Lake Malawi in the 1980s by the Australian oil firm Swala Energy, which estimated that there are 4 billion barrels of oil under the lake. The lake has been split into six blocks for exploration and contracts were given to several companies from the United Arab Emirates and the United Kingdom. Nature conservationists have protested against the licensing and potential drilling of oil to UNESCO, as the lake is one of its protected World Heritage sites. Plummeting oil prices have reduced the impetus to start drilling, though it is expected that the projects will go ahead and could drastically change Malawi's economy.

Telecoms

Telecommunications is a fast-growing sector in Malawi. There are two cell phone companies—Airtel and TNM Limited—but two landline companies— Access and Malawi Telecommunications Limited— offer cell phone handsets for their areas of coverage. A third cell phone company has yet to roll out its services. Cell phone coverage is wide, despite the high tariff costs.

Banking

The Standard Bank and National Bank of Malawi dominate the market, though emerging banks, such as Opportunity International, First Merchant Bank, NBS Bank, and FDH Bank, which bought a majority stake of the former state-owned Malawi Savings Bank, have extensive networks targeting rural communities. Competition in the sector is compounded by micro-finance village banking groups, which now offer loans without collateral.

Most Malawians still work outside the formal financial sector, being neither taxed nor monitored by the government.

Economic Outlook

Malawi enjoys a stable and democratic government, and continues to implement a program agreed by the International Monetary Fund that tracks economic performance based on key targets.

In 2017, the economy grew by 2.4 percent, with inflation down to single digits, and though growth in 2018 was projected to rise to between 4 and 6 percent it is likely to go down as vast areas of maize have been affected by army worms.

Weak fiscal discipline in Malawi has been a core driver of macroeconomic instability in recent years. A public financial management scandal in 2013 triggered sharp reductions in the level of on-budget development assistance received from various donors. Public service reforms are being undertaken to deliver efficiency and curb corruption and fraud, which drain one-third of public finances.

Poverty and inequality remain stubbornly high in Malawi. The 2010/11 Integrated Household Survey showed that more than half the population was poor and one-quarter lived in extreme poverty. This is mainly due to low agricultural productivity, which should change as investment is focused on irrigation and proper land management.

The anti-smoking lobby is threatening Malawi's tobacco industry, which has seen farmers receive poor prices. Other crops, such as tea, coffee, and cotton, have also been affected by low prices, and changes in the quota regime for preferential markets for sugar by the European Union could all have an impact on the economy.

Diversification into agro-processing and the tourism and mining sectors promises to be Malawi's quickest way to raise its economic profile.

MALAWI IN AFRICA AND BEYOND

Malawi is a founding member of the fourteen-nation Southern Africa Development Community, which includes the regional economic powerhouse South Africa. It is also a founding member of Africa's largest trading block, the Common Market for East and Southern Africa (COMESA).

Malawi, a beacon of peace in the region, gave sanctuary to more than a million refugees from the Mozambican civil war, and continues to host thousands of refugees and asylum seekers from the war-torn Democratic Republic of the Congo (DRC), Burundi, Somalia, Eritrea, and Ethiopia.

Its military, the Malawi Defence Force, is renowned for its professionalism and discipline and has been a major player in United Nations Peace Keeping missions to Ivory Coast, Darfur in Sudan, Liberia, and the DRC. It has also served on emergency rescue operations in Mozambique during major flooding.

Politically, Malawian leaders have a close relationship with Zambia, which evolves depending on the occupant of State House, while the former Zimbabwean leader, Robert Mugabe, enjoyed close relationships with all Malawi's leaders and attended the inaugurations of all Malawi's presidents after each election.

Malawi's founding president, Hastings Kamuzu Banda, had a frosty relationship with the African Union's predecessor, the Organization of African Unity, whose summits he only attended twice, and opted for closer cooperation with Portuguese Mozambique and apartheid South Africa. He was deeply mistrusted by Mozambique's ruling Frelimo Party, who accused him of arming the Renamo rebels.

Interestingly, after the anti-apartheid icon Nelson Mandela was released from prison, among the first countries he visited was Malawi, where he thanked Banda for his financial support of the African National Congress during the struggle.

Banda was particularly close to Kenya's founding president, Jomo Kenyatta. For years Kenyatta's statue at Kwacha International Conference Centre was the only one in Malawi, until third president Bingu wa Mutharika erected a statue to Banda in Lilongwe. The Kenyan and Malawian flags have similar colors, differing only in the central image.

Banda, a strong capitalist, distrusted Tanzania's first president, Julius Nyerere, who played host to dissidents, critical of his regime, who were fleeing from Malawi. The two countries have a long-running dispute over the borderline on Lake Malawi, and both sides cite the Heligoland Treaty of 1890 between Great Britain and Germany. The wrangle arose when, after they had captured Tanganyika from Germany, the British colonial government placed the waters of the lake under a single jurisdiction, that of the territory of Nyasaland, without a separate administration for the Tanganyikan portion. The dispute came to a head in 1967, when Tanzania officially protested to Malawi. In 2012, Malawi's oil exploration initiative brought the issue to the fore, with Tanzania demanding that exploration cease until the dispute was settled.

Banda's foreign policy included recognition of Taiwan, as he was staunchly anti-communist.

Banda's successor tried to position Malawi as a peacemaker, brokering the historic first face-to-face meetings between the DRC's President Laurent Kabila and Rwanda's President Paul Kagame, and later between Sudanese President Omar Al Bashir and his southern opponent John Garang. Muluzi's peace attempts extended to Burundi, where he later struck up a close friendship with then President Pierre Buyoya, who has remained a frequent visitor to Malawi. Muluzi was very close to Zambia's presidents Fredrick Chiluba and Michael Sata and Libya's Muammar Gaddafi, who traveled to Malawi in 2002.

Bingu wa Mutharika developed a new eastward-looking foreign policy that saw Malawi switch to the People's Republic of China and opened embassies in all the BRICS nations except for Russia. He developed a pan-African stature and served as the first Malawian president to chair the African Union. He advocated state subsidy of agriculture and African economic independence. He died in office in 2012.

His successor, Joyce Banda, who became president by constitutional order, advanced the cause of women in politics and was close to Africa's first female president, Liberian leader Ellen Johnson Sirleaf, AU chair Nkosazana Dlamini Zuma, and the then US secretary of state, Hillary Clinton. Joyce Banda lost the elections in 2014.

Peter Mutharika, who was elected president in 2014, has concentrated mainly on domestic issues, with most of his international focus on trade and investment, the United Nations, and regional trading blocs. His passion has been wildlife conservation. He has ordered the burning of more than US $4 million worth of ivory confiscated from poachers and strengthened the anti-poaching laws. The former professor at Washington Law School has welcomed negotiations with Tanzania, but has ruled out giving in to its demand for an equal share of the Lake.

Outside Africa, Scotland and Malawi have the closest relations; there have been thousands of exchange programs over the 159 years since David Livingstone arrived at Lake Malawi in 1859. The two nations enjoy cooperation in education, health, politics, social development, and cultural exchanges, and, as we have seen, Malawi's commercial capital, Blantyre, is named after Livingstone's birthplace.

Malawians are renowned in the region for their hard work and honesty, and they constitute the largest foreign labor force in South Africa, from the mining sector to medical professionals, as well as in Zimbabwe and Zambia.

chapter two

VALUES & ATTITUDES

THE MALAWIAN CHARACTER

The Malawians are, by and large, honest, conservative, good-humored, and mild-tempered. They tend to be quiet—though they like poking their noses into other people's business—and are always smiling. Those smiles, at the ready even when they are in deep poverty, and even when they are in trouble with the authorities, have been a source of debate, anger, and sometimes misinterpretation. Their neighbors in Zambia and Zimbabwe considered them "sleepy" or "backward" until they became the first country in the former Federation of Rhodesia and Nyasaland to rebel against their colonial masters. Many call them ignorant and deeply superstitious.

The Malawian traits of discipline, hard work, and perseverance come from a long tradition of strict social discipline that is imparted from birth. It includes respect for all elders and near godlike reverence toward authority. Chiefs and leaders of all kinds, including church leaders, are shown and accorded the utmost reverence.

Children learn to fear and respect anyone older than themselves, and women are taught at a young age that they should fear and obey their husbands. These attitudes are implanted at different stages of life, but the most important time for this is at puberty, when both girls and boys undergo community counseling.

For strangers, this strict disciplinary code translates into warmth and helpfulness. Visitors are welcomed with open arms and offered meals, and, where required, a typical Malawian village as a community will host or help a total stranger. The legendary hospitality of Malawians, despite their poverty, is well known to Southern Africans who have visited or worked in Malawi.

COMMUNAL LIFE

A well-rounded culture of discipline, honesty, and hard work involves the sharing of successes and challenges as a community. This sharing, however, is something that a stranger might find difficult to understand. Malawian life is communal from the start, and later involves the sharing of houses by age groups, and women doing chores together; literally every aspect of life is shared with neighbors and friends, to such an extent that the members of the community have very few secrets from each other.

This "sharing" can take the form of discussing anything—from sexual performance to financial affairs—or the giving of advice, which, even unsolicited, most Malawians are likely to offer to anyone they think needs their help or direction. It is important to remember that most of them assume it is their duty to help anyone whom they consider to be in need.

GENDER AND SEXUALITY

Religion, mainly Christianity and Islam, has been influential in Malawi for the past century. Society is strongly patriarchal. In all the major tribes men dominate even the day-to-day lives of women. Men are largely expected to be breadwinners and women homemakers. Domestic violence has been covered up for years, with young girls entering marriage being counseled to believe in a philosophy of *banja ndikupilira* ("marriage is perseverance") that has led to years of women's suffering in silence. The counseling sessions of brides center mainly on how to please men, and foster the creation of semi-slave conditions for housewives.

Gender inequality in Malawian society is clearly evident in the distribution of labor, where in formal employment women's wages are low, and domestically the women work longer hours than their male counterparts. In the villages, a woman typically wakes around 3:00 to 4:00 a.m. every day, works with her husband in the field, and returns home by 6:00 a.m. to prepare breakfast for the children—and this could include a long walk to fetch fresh water from a well. She then goes out to gather firewood and returns to prepare and serve food for lunch, clears up, and does the housework, before starting preparations for the evening meal. Women are the first to rise, and the last to sleep. Men will also work hard, but for fewer hours.

The domestic routine closely reflects the gender roles in Malawian society, which consigns women to a purely supporting role. Women in offices, despite having a female president for two years (2012–14), are

largely underpaid and the few token senior positions that have been occupied remain below 5 percent, in a country whose population is 60 percent female.

From ancient times, Malawian men have had many wives, and until the introduction of Christianity and as late as the 1970s it was generally acceptable for a man to marry more than one wife. Polygamy is now prohibited by law, despite some religions recognizing it. Most men keep concubines, and extramarital affairs continue to flourish in both urban and rural settings.

The role of women, apart from looking after their families, includes managing births, weddings, and funerals. Politically, very few women have made it to public office; the majority, in the name of traditional culture, are confined to singing praises and dancing for their male counterparts.

In this deeply religious nation a few Churches, such as the dominant Church of Central Africa Presbyterian (CCAP), have started ordaining female ministers. They are very few in number, but this could go a long way to addressing the critical gender imbalance in all areas of society, which for decades has been shaped by the biblical preaching of "Wives, submit yourselves unto your own husbands," and that cultural philosophy that "marriage is perseverance." These two phrases encapsulate the way that sexuality has been the main driver of the gender imbalance: women, especially the majority in the rural population, continue to be expected only to please their husbands. Foreign women will find that Malawian men like domination, and frown at an independent-minded woman.

DRESS

Only in recent times has traditional African attire, especially the colorful *chitenje* prints, seen a revival after years of Westernized dressing. Women are expected to wear long skirts covering their knees, and in the villages, must add the *chitenje* (wrapper) to be considered properly covered. These wrappers are also recommended for tourists, particularly because, in some areas, such as urban markets, Western-syle short skirts and tight pants are frowned upon.

The strict dress code was legislated by Malawi's first president, Hastings Kamuzu Banda. The law ensured that, for men, the English gentleman's dress—suit, shirt, and tie—was adopted and adhered to in all public offices. This law, repealed at the dawn of multiparty democracy, prohibited baggy pants, long hair, and any unconventional styles for men, while women could be arrested for wearing miniskirts, pants, and revealing garments.

How one dresses now depends on where one is and how comfortable one would feel in certain situations. Along the lakeshores or in the tourist centers there are no dress codes or restrictions, but, as stated above, female tourists wearing revealing clothes might be disapproved of, and hear whistles or jeers.

The only traditional attire for Malawian women is basically a three-piece set of blouse, long skirt, and matching headgear called a *duku*. For men, a safari suit, usually a short-sleeved shirt and matching trousers, is said to be traditional dress, though these were borrowed from East Africa. Colorful printed shirts, made from the same cotton as women's *chitenje*, have become acceptable, especially among the younger generation.

In 2016 the government decreed that on Fridays public servants should wear Malawian dress as part of promoting local industry, and it has helped to popularize the men's fashion trend. However, for business, church, and other formal events the convention remains the British formal dress for both men and women. Churches remain sensitive to dressing, and if you are planning to attend a service it is important to check what is appropriate with

A Quick Change

Dr. Hastings Kamuzu Banda's eccentric dress code is well known in Namibia, where Banda used to charter Air Namibia's 747 planes for his annual month-long vacations in the UK. The plane would be repainted in Air Malawi colors, but the hostesses were all Namibians. One year they landed in Malawi wearing uniforms with short skirts that showed their knees. The Malawi government officials were mortified that the "Lion of Malawi," as Banda was called, would be flying with such women. They were ordered to remain on board, and tailors from the Malawi Young Pioneers (a paramilitary group disguised as a youth training program) were quickly dispatched to the airport with a pile of traditional cotton wrappers. The women were all soon wearing long skirts printed with Banda's face. During the flight, one unfortunate hostess tripped over her long skirt and nearly bumped into Malawi's feared leader. One of his bodyguards leaped forward and caught her in the nick of time.

the relevant church; some, especially the Seventh Day Adventists, still ban pants for women in favor of skirts.

THE EXTENDED FAMILY AND COMMUNITY SHARING

Mwana wa nzako, ngwako yemwe, ukachenjera manja udya naye ("A neighbor's child is yours as well; treat him nicely—he'll remember you.") This is the core philosophy of the communal life that exists among Malawians. A child is the responsibility of everyone, and each village thinks of itself as one big family. Children are taught their family tree, and to respect and help their neighbors. Within communal living the rules are very simple: neighbors, friends, and relations turn up unannounced, and you welcome them with a smile. Almost everyone is "related" in some way to the next person—literally related, through family or marriage, or connected by school or church, or through parents or grandparents living or working together.

Responsibility for looking after the elderly or any orphans in the village falls on everyone. The old ones enjoy the companionship, and being looked after by the whole village, and children from other families are expected to help by cooking, cleaning, fetching, and carrying.

There are only two homes for elderly people in Malawi, and these are basically filled by foreign nationals who have made the country their home. Orphans are normally taken in by their relations or, in urban areas, community social organizations that have orphanages. While the legal system provides for adoption, most children are raised by families who regard them as their own without going through the formal adoption process.

Girls, especially in the villages, are expected to help their neighbors when they draw water or go to the maize mill; boys are expected to help during harvest and with other chores around the household, including herding animals. An adult who sees a

friend's child misbehaving can reprimand and report him or her to the parents—and not all claims of "relationship" refer to blood relations; they might just be neighbors. If you have something that your neighbors don't have, or that they need, you can be asked to lend it, or you can offer its use, without expecting payment of any kind; it is your obligation as a good neighbor, or as a member of the extended family, to help them.

In urban centers, there is a mixture of traditional and Western communal living.

RESPECT AND DISCIPLINE

In all areas of the country, older people expect anyone younger than themselves, including foreigners, to show them respect. That includes not looking someone older than yourself in the eye. How you hold yourself is important: never speak to anyone with your hands in your pockets; using hand gestures is also considered rude in some circumstances. Hats should be removed when approaching or being in the presence of others. The young should wait for adults to speak first, and not argue. In the villages, women still often kneel when speaking to men, to their elders and in-laws, and to influential people within the community.

Amusingly, much of this can be reversed during a social outing if the person sponsoring it has more money than the rest. They become a "wise man," or "elder," and are accorded respect even by the elders to whom otherwise they would be paying respects.

At social events women are expected to remain in the company of other women, and men with fellow men. In some churches, too, this is still the practice, with men and women sitting on different sides. In towns and urban centers, however, behavior depends more on one's views and not necessarily on tradition.

RELIGIOUS TOLERANCE

Malawi is one of the most peaceful countries, and religion has never been a source of conflict. The two major religions, Christianity and Islam, happily coexist, and in some places, such as Mangochi and Balaka, mosques and churches are side by side. Due

to intermarriages and mixed communal lifestyle, it is difficult to imagine neighbors fighting each other over religious differences.

Religious tolerance is particularly evident in the fact that a majority Christian population has elected a Muslim president twice and a vice president once.

WORLD VIEWS, TRADITIONAL AND MODERN

Contemporary Malawi is a mix of tradition and modernity. The majority of people are both deeply religious and superstitious. The coexistence of two distinct spiritual worlds means that most people believe in God and at the same time hold on to their traditional beliefs and superstitions.

Religious views have shaped Malawian attitudes toward certain countries, especially those seen as promoting homosexuality and abortion. Homosexuality is illegal, and widely regarded by all Churches as a sin. The constitution's Bill of Rights prohibits discrimination on sexual grounds, but religious and cultural bodies remain solidly opposed to any attempt to legitimize homosexuality. In 2010 two young men who publicly entered a traditional engagement were arrested and sentenced to fourteen years' imprisonment. Civil society has encouraged debate on minority rights, but the topic is sensitive and most Malawians condemn any suggestion that homosexual behavior is acceptable or normal. However, there is no reported threat to gays, save when they express themselves openly.

However, most young people now embrace American culture, and the explosion of social media has generated a new hybrid view on everything from politics to fashion and music. The conservative religious influence is always evident during debates on controversial issues, and all ages seem to agree on their belief-based views. The traditional view is now waning, and Malawians are more aware of global issues—from the election of Donald Trump to soccer transfers in the English and Spanish Football Leagues. For anyone interacting with a Malawian, politics and sports are dominant topics, apart from religion.

ATTITUDES TOWARD TIME

For most official business time is of the essence, but at times the "position of the sun" still matters more to many. Life is usually slow-paced in the villages, where most activities take place during daylight hours because the majority of people have no electricity.

Punctuality is not in the Malawian nature, and being even an hour late is acceptable. However, first-time foreign businesspeople should arrive at a meeting at least five minutes early, to create a good impression.

In most offices, the first hour of the day is spent catching up on current affairs and checking in with each other, so that the real business, other than in banks and the more commercially oriented shops and organizations, starts about an hour after opening. The same trend even affects hospitals and public services where, despite the official opening time being 7:30 a.m., most services don't start to run on full capacity until around 8:30 a.m. It is important to be early for services that require waiting in line, and to have patience until one's turn. Protesting, or reporting of delays to supervisors, will only see one being ignored or delayed further.

Though most establishments offer an hour's lunch break, an average "lunch hour" lasts no less than two hours! The best possible time for an afternoon appointment is around 2:00 p.m. Normally, the more senior the person, the longer the lunch hour. After 3:30 p.m. it is rare for a client to be seen unless in the case of an emergency or a required service. Most workers will already be thinking of the next day, and the business winds down until closing time.

ATTITUDES TOWARD WORK
Malawians are hardworking and honest. In the villages, farming involves manual labor, using a traditional hoe, and can take many hours each day.

The typical farmer rises around 4:00 a.m. and works on his land until the heat becomes too great, around 10:00 a.m., then takes a break, and returns around 3:00 p.m. Most farmers supplement their crops with garden produce and the rearing of livestock. Time is shared between the activities.

In urban areas, the majority of people work in industry, in offices, and as market traders. Their honesty and their loyalty to their employers have earned Malawians a solid reputation, and they have become the most sought-after workers in regional markets. Most who work in the formal sector use their income to support their extended families.

RESOURCEFULNESS AND THRIFT
A true Malawian never throws anything away. If you fry something and have left-over oil, you keep it for the next thing you fry. The same goes for many other things, including tires. So, if your company

buys a new car, after two years it will replace the tires. A good Malawian will use them on his own car for another two years, then sell them to a tire dealer who will either sell them on to someone who will use them on an ox-cart or make rubber bands to be used to bundle items or tie wooden fences. The rest can be used to make the so-called "Jesus sandals." After the end of the Jesus sandal you cut it up to use it as a support for your door handle; it will end its life only when you use it in the fire to smoke out bees and harvest their honey.

ATTITUDES TOWARD WEALTH

Malawians who have a genuine desire to move out of poverty admire people who are wealthy. The wealthy, especially those whose wealth is traceable, are part of their community and are readily accepted and respected. However, unexplained riches always attract gossip, in both urban and rural areas. Recent financial scandals involving public finances have raised suspicions among Malawians about how certain individuals have acquired their wealth. Nevertheless, those who are rich and philanthropic are heartily welcomed, as they donate to social causes and churches and are part of the community.

TRIBAL RELATIONS AND INDIVIDUAL IDENTITY

In Malawi, tribalism crops up mainly in the context of politics. For ordinary people, from the home to

"GET-RICH-QUICK" MYTHS

Very wealthy people may be the subject of widespread gossip about money gained by magical means, or through Satanic cults, or by outright theft. "Get rich quick" stories have created various myths and accusations that have destroyed some of the most prominent people in society. Some, if not most, of these have come from business rivals, angry dumped mistresses, and people who are simply jealous of the wealthy. In the villages, allegations can range from that of owning a large snake that goes about at night swallowing money in shops to that of killing people using black magic to boost business.

A number of cases of mysterious murders of women and men and the removal of their body parts, and more recently of persons with albinism, are all attributed to the get-rich-quick myths in a society that is overly superstitious. People believe that mixing charms with human bones or body parts can help one to become rich. In most instances, the body parts never find a market, and the smell of rotting flesh leads to discovery of the evil deed before a buyer can be found. Essentially, save for a few crooked witch doctors, who deny involvement and disappear, or hope one will fail to find the parts, there is really no market for any body parts.

the workplace, tribe rarely matters and it's not a common topic. Most complaints about tribalism occur within the political setup and are related more to political patronage and regions of origin than to actual tribes.

Malawian presidents have a delicate job of trying to appoint people from different regions, tribes, and religions if they want to be acceptable to all. This has led to parties pairing a presidential candidate and running mate from two different administrative regions, with the south having emerged victorious in the last five elections due to its larger population. Regionalism and tribalism are exaggerated by those seeking to gain political capital; in fact, many Malawians have intermarried, and the development of large tobacco, tea, cotton, coffee, and timber plantations has led to the internal migration of people of different tribes who form new communities with no cultural alignment.

ATTITUDES TOWARD FOREIGNERS

Subconsciously, attitudes toward foreigners are mainly formed by the nationality of the foreigner, and most such attitudes are the result of years of interaction. Africans, especially those from Nigeria, are viewed with suspicion, though many have married locals in what are known as "visa marriages"—marriages to acquire residence permits. Readily acceptable African foreigners include those from the East and Southern African nations, such as Zambia, Rwanda, Burundi, Zimbabwe, Botswana, and South Africa. Apart from being trade neighbors, Tanzania and Mozambique are famed for their light-skinned women, whom many black men think particularly beautiful.

White people are *Nzungu* (white person), whether they are from the USA, Canada, Germany, France, the UK, or Australia; the only exceptions are the Portuguese, mainly due to many coming from Mozambique who are called by the local name *Apwitikizi*, and white South Africans, whose corrupted local name for Boer is *Mb'uno*. Asians, predominantly from the Indian subcontinent, are called *Amwenye*, and they dominate the retail and wholesale trade, with many accepted as locals. Only the Chinese are referred to directly by their nationality—Chinese. The best-loved foreigners include missionaries, medical personnel, and teachers who have settled in rural areas, and the Peace Corps (USA), Japanese, and British VSO workers, who normally make a good impression with their efforts to speak, eat, and live in local communities.

Malawi is a home to many refugees who are fleeing from conflicts in the Great Lakes region, and its warmth has seen many settle down and call the country home. Malawians have elected white members of parliament, including two of Dutch origin—Jan Jaap Sonke (1999–2004), who became a deputy cabinet minister, and Jacqueline Kouwenhoven (2014–19); one of Israeli origin—David Bisnowaty (2014–19); and one naturalized Malawian—the late Harold Williams, a human rights activist who died in 2011.

CUSTOMS & TRADITIONS

THE ROLE OF THE CHIEF

Malawi is a mixture of the old and the new, and traditional leaders encompass both. Paramount chiefs and traditional leaders sit on modern local government councils; they used to preside over their own courts, which they still do but with limited powers. They directly or indirectly own all tribal land, which, until the colonial declaration of a protectorate in 1891, belonged to them in totality.

The largest tribe is the Chewa, who call their highest-ranking chief "Chalo," which means "land."

The Ngoni, who emigrated from South Africa, call theirs "Nkhosi ya Makhosi" for the Jele clan in northern Malawi and "Inkosi ya Makosi" for the Maseko clan in the central region, which translates as "King of Kings." Their powers now include holding traditional courts for conducting marriages, funerals, and birth rites, and adjudicating in land matters in their area. The traditional structure entails total obedience from the subjects, and most succession is through the bloodline, which for Chewa is matrilineal, through the son of the chief's sister, and for the Ngoni and others the first-born of the chief.

Looking After One's Own

The belief among the Chewa is that a man is responsible for his sister's children, who constitute the true bloodline of the family. This originates in the suspicion that wives may deceive their husbands about the paternity of their children, but that one's sister cannot lie about her own child. This ancient practice continues to this very day.

Chiefs occupy very important roles in day-to-day life, though very few—like Inkosi ya Makosi Gomani—are known to have fought against the colonial administration. Successive governments exploited them, introducing special payments and favors, and using them to speak against government critics. Most of the urban population view chiefs as partisan, bending toward the ruling party, and don't accord them much respect. At the local level in the rural areas, however—where the hierarchy starts with the village headman, goes on to the group village headman or woman, the sub-traditional authority, and then on to the full traditional authority who looks after a wide area—the authority of the chief remains absolute. It is important for visitors to rural areas, especially those going on public engagements or for projects, to make contact with the chief and introduce themselves.

"Traditional Philosophy"

One of the most fascinating aspects of Malawian culture is the use of myths to control people's basic everyday behavior. These include, for example, denying a pregnant woman's craving for eggs by saying that eating eggs could harm the baby—yet the real reason is to protect chicken production. The young are warned against taking the traditional "Viagra" roots known as *gondolosi*, with the threat of developing oversized private parts if they do so. This "traditional philosophy" is so obviously controlling that at times it is clearly necessary to take such warnings with a pinch of salt.

CULTURAL FESTIVALS

Traditional festivals used to be village-based and mainly related to specific occasions. Now they are becoming bigger and more widely promoted, resuscitating the once fading cultures.

January

The Tonga celebrate their Chilimika festival to welcome the new year.

March

The Ngoni of Mchinji hold their Ncwala event in the neighboring Zambian town of Chipata, under Inkosi ya Makosi Mpezeni, to celebrate the first harvests.

August

The most multicultural event is Kungoni Open Day, held on the first Saturday in August at the Kungoni Centre of Culture and Art at Mua, in Dedza. The center is run by a Canadian Catholic priest, who has built an impressive museum of the Chewa, Ngoni, Yao, and Matengo cultures of the area.

In mid-August the Tumbuka who are under Chief Katumbi celebrate their cultural identity with traditional dances in the Mulindafwa ceremony.

The last weekend of August is reserved for Central and Southern Africa's largest cultural festival, as the Chewa trek to Mkaika, about 43 miles (70 km) into eastern Zambia from the Malawi border, using the Chipata road. The ceremony, held after the harvest, is another parliament for Chewa people, when different Chewa chiefs from Zambia, Malawi, and Mozambique present reports or grievances to Chewa King Kalonga Gawa Undi. The name Kalonga means "the one who installs subordinate chiefs." Gawa means "the one who gives out land," and Undi means "the one who protects the subordinates." The ceremony was banned by the colonial authorities in 1934, but Kalonga Gawa Undi Chivunga revived it in 1984. The Chewa Nyau dance, Gule Wamkulu, which was officially recognized by UNESCO in 2006, dominates the festival. The energetic Nyau dancers, referred to as *virombo* (wild

animal spirits) in Chewa, are initiated men who wear special costumes and masks made of wood and straw, representing characters from the world of the spirits and the dead. More than a hundred Gule Wamkulu characters take part in the three-day carnival.

The Jele Ngoni of Mzimba hold their Umtheto in mid-August at Hora Mountain, where they defeated the Tumbukas when they first came into the district. The word *umtheto* literally means a rule or procedure for solving a problem, but this event is basically a people's session for the Jele Ngoni, and is celebrated with meat, beer, and dance.

September

The Mseko Ngoni of Ntcheu, who are more colorful, hold their Umhlangano wa Maseko ("Meeting of the Maseko") in early September. Inkosi ya Makosi Gomani (now the fifth) presides over the festival.

The Tumbuka under Chief Chikulamayembe hold their Gonapamuhanya ("He who sleeps in the sun") on the last weekend of September. Politics has seen Chikulamayembe elevated to paramount chief, a contradiction of Tumbuka culture, in which chieftainship is based on families and clans.

October

Another major festival is the Mulhako wa Lhomwe, which marks the end of the annual cultural festivals in Malawi and is held in late October at Chonde in Mulanje district. It was started in 2011, and has since grown into a must-see event.

There are other exciting cultural ceremonies in all districts. These include Malipenga and Vimbuza dancing across the North and lakeshore areas, and Gule Wamkulu dancers are always a prominent feature along the intercity road. Because of the strict rule that children must be back in school after holidays, festivals celebrating the passage to adulthood (*chinamwali, jando, dambwe*) after the

initiation period are held in August, and it is common in most districts to see a group of women and colorfully dressed young people dancing and heading for parties. All festivals are open to everyone, although some areas, such as the Gule Wamkulu initiation camps, are out of bounds to visitors.

PUBLIC HOLIDAYS

Public holidays in Malawi have four political, one cultural, honoring mothers, New Year's Day, Labour Day, and five religious holidays, spread across the year. The political holidays, save for March 3 and July 6, have been a source of intense debate, and, depending on current politics, they can be removed or have their dates changed. Mothers' Day and Kamuzu Day have in the past two decades been changed or removed.

January 1	New Year's Day
January 15	John Chilembwe Day
March 3	Martyrs' Day
Good Friday	
Easter Monday	
May 1	Labour Day
May 14	Kamuzu Day
July 6	Independence Day
October 15	Mothers' Day
Sighting The New Moon in the Month Of Ramadan	Eidi Ul Fitri
December 25	Christmas Day
December 26	Boxing Day

GREETINGS AND COURTESY

Greetings are an elaborate ceremony in Malawi.
Respect and decorum should always be observed.
You are expected to shake hands, and not hug. The
key point is to be aware in advance of the status or
seniority of the person you are meeting, and to
address them appropriately. The host, or the more
important person, leads the greeting. So, in the
case of meeting a chief, a man should show respect
by making a slight bow, and a woman should bend
her knees, with her hands clasped together. The
senior person will either say a greeting or extend
his hand and ask some questions. The greeting can
be long and elaborate: you can be asked who you are,
what you do, and even about your family. Smile, and
wait until you receive a signal that the greeting and
questions are over, and then respond. In visiting a
chief's court, or at any special event, you are
expected to express gratitude for the warm welcome
you are receiving and to report on how you have
traveled.

Though slightly different in urban areas, the
procedure for a formal meeting could almost fall
into the same pattern—greeting individuals as soon
as you arrive, and taking time to chat about other
things. More importantly, you should address people
by their titles if you are aware of them. In the case
of educated people, or even those with honorary
titles, find out if they are a professor or a doctor,
and address them accordingly. Politicians expect
full address of "Honorable," or "Right Honorable,"
or "Your Excellency" as a sign of respect and

recognition. The titles should be used even in
informal settings.

BIRTH AND BAPTISM

Childbirth in Malawi is a very important cultural
and religious event. Pregnant women are subject to
stringent rules, some based on tradition, others on
conservative religious views. Girls or women who
become pregnant outside marriage are considered
to have loose morals, and usually traditional
engagement ceremonies are hurriedly organized by
parents to avoid tarnishing the family name.

Health care services now include obligatory
hospital deliveries and prenatal counseling, but older
women retain the responsibility of guiding young ones
during pregnancy. Even in a case where a wife and
mother-in-law treat each other as rivals, pregnancy
dilutes the rivalry. Churches, too, have now started
"women counseling" sessions to ensure that strict
moral conduct is followed. Modest dress—meaning
a long gown and a traditional wrapper (*chitenje*)—
is considered appropriate for pregnancy. Urban
women prefer pants with loose blouses, though this
still raises eyebrows.

When a child is born in a village, the whole village
is informed, and it is a joyous occasion. Everyone in
the village, or even visiting, is expected to join the early
visitors to the hospital or at the home of the newborn to
congratulate the parents. For most Christians, babies are
baptized within months or a year after birth, and this is
another colorful event not to be missed.

Tsempho

Realizing that men might look elsewhere during their wives' pregnancy, or after the birth, elderly women counselors concocted a link between a newborn and the father. It is called *tsempho*, and the literal translation is "parallel." Men are told that having sex away from home when their wife is pregnant, or soon after giving birth, will cause the child to fall sick and/or die. This belief has led to some men being accused of causing the death, and stoned, if their baby died while they were away traveling. To this day, men still fear *tsempho* so much that most remain faithful, afraid of being accused of causing harm to their child

MARRIAGE

Marriage in Malawi is a perfect mix of tradition and modernity, culture and religion. There are three basic stages: the proposal, the traditional engagement, and the wedding. In all tribes, the groom's family members, led by an uncle, conduct the proposal stage. The most important step in the procedure is when they meet the bride's parents or family and ask for her hand in marriage. Though an urban couple will start with the type of proposal and agreement between the two of them that is common in the West, no wedding in Malawi can take place without their families meeting and agreeing to it. For tribes such as the Sena, Ngoni, Tonga, Tumbuka, and Ngonde, the proposal stage includes the negotiation of the bride price, or dowry. Bride prices have been spiraling upward, and,

if families don't like the tribe or the family of the suitor, ridiculously high prices may be proposed.

After agreement is reached, the second stage is the engagement. This can take place a month, a year, or two years before the actual wedding. It has now turned into a colorful event, and includes the sharing of chicken, welcoming each other's families, and counseling the couple. After this, by tradition, they are considered to be married, and the man can visit or stay with the woman at any point, nobody minding if the two share a bedroom. In some cases, if the bride becomes pregnant before the wedding, the engagement becomes, in effect, the marriage.

The final stage is the wedding—a hugely costly affair that takes weeks or months to prepare. The evening before, the women cook, the men drink, and the kids play music all night long. The day starts with a religious ceremony, and the reception —a celebration not to be missed—takes place in the afternoon or evening. Everyone dresses up in their Sunday best, enjoys the food and music, and showers the newlyweds with money.

Foreigners marrying a Malawian are expected to undergo all the rituals. Most Malawians marrying foreigners do so outside the country, but still bring them home for a traditional Malawian wedding.

Those wishing to avoid the hullabaloo can simply register their marriage legally at the District Commissioner's office.

Prenuptial agreements are not yet recognized in Malawi. Divorce is acceptable through the courts or the chief's proclamation in villages. The marriageable age until 2016 was fifteen with parental consent, but it was then raised to eighteen. Polygamy is illegal, though concubines with children resulting from the relationship, or who have cohabited for a certain period, can claim support from the man.

FUNERALS

Death is the most feared event. It also brings out deep-rooted superstitious beliefs in most Malawians. Nobody dies without a reason. Suspicious deaths— which include accidents, death from lightning strikes, and sometimes even from strokes or heart attacks—are all attributed to witchcraft. Funerals therefore attract large crowds, and communities frown on those who don't come to share in sorrowful occasions. Neighbors are expected to attend, open their homes, and not go anywhere except in support of the bereaved family.

Women cook food, and everyone is expected to partake when invited. A whole cow, for those with means, may be slaughtered. From the day of the death, people are expected to come and sleep at the funeral home, and there will be vigils, with hymns if the deceased was a believer. The day of burial, the

THE CHIEF'S FUNERAL

In all tribes the chief's funeral is treated differently from other people's. The Chewa traditional ceremony is led by the Gule Wamkulu religious brotherhood, and secret rites, including the ritual Nyau dance, are observed. Before this ceremony there is a formal memorial service at the home of the deceased. Owing to the sensitivity of the Gule Wamkulu ceremony, protocol requires that outsiders attend the earlier service only.

The Tumbuka bury their chiefs at night, so people are asked to leave after the funeral service, while the coffin is outside the grave. Interment takes place later, attended only by chiefs.

The Ngoni are more colorful, and have a longer mourning. Traditionally they bury their chiefs (though it used to be everyone) seated. The belief is that kings don't die; they just sleep. In the past, the dead king's possessions were buried with him for his use in the afterlife. This has now been reduced to essential personal effects.

actual funeral day, is normally one or two days after the death. In Malawi people are buried quickly, as it is believed that the spirits will get angry if the body is kept longer. The typical funeral service will be a church sermon or Islamic teaching, and then burial at a cemetery. Most people wish their remains to be taken back to their home villages, and companies or employers are expected to meet all related costs and grant paid leave to workers attending funerals or accompanying the body to the village.

People passing a mourning house, or a graveyard being prepared for burial, must show respect by not wearing hats, riding bicycles, or playing music. If you meet a funeral procession when driving, you are expected to slow down, or stop and get out of your vehicle, as a sign of respect to the dead. A fine is payable by anyone contravening these rules.

WITCHCRAFT AND SUPERNATURAL BELIEFS

Religion and older traditions sit side-by-side in Malawi. Most people are Christians or Muslims, but they still hold on to their traditional beliefs. These range from birth, where traditional birth attendants used to hold more sway than hospitals, to death, where in most cases a witch is said to be involved.

Malawians are likely to visit a traditional doctor (also called a witch doctor) in the same way as they would a Western medical practitioner. Mysterious wealth is attributed to magic, and religious leaders with growing churches are often suspected of having used magic to entice people into their congregations.

Such beliefs have led to shocking incidents of people's private parts or breasts being cut off, and to attacks on albinos for their body parts, for the making of wealth creation charms.

Old people have been stoned to death on being suspected as witches, and stories have been told about vampires sucking people's blood, turning into cats, and running away.

These beliefs are so deeply rooted that it is impossible to reason with many followers. Even Churches have failed to eradicate the practice of visiting witch doctors, which they regard as a sin. The witch doctors now advertise publicly, and operate next to hospitals, patients leaving their hospital beds for consultations. It is better for the visitor to stay away from witchcraft debates—people tend to become emotional, as they hold their beliefs so dear.

Some tribes and areas are feared to have supernatural powers, while others are said to have produced protection charms. Districts such as Mulanje, Nsanje, Machinga, Ntchisi, Rumphi, and Karonga are listed as havens for witchdoctors.

HARMFUL CULTURAL PRACTICES

At her most vulnerable point, after her husband's death, a woman was expected to have sex with a man from her husband's family to "cleanse" her and appease the spirits, while in some cultures, such as the Tumbuka, she was expected to go for *chokolo*, where the husband's relation would marry her. Among the Sena, girls reaching puberty were subjected to sex with an adult male to initiate them into adulthood. Among the Chewa, widows were asked to leave everything and were expelled from the village in an act known as *kusudzula* ("unpeeled"), after which they were free to remarry. Boys after attending initiation ceremonies were encouraged to find a woman to prove their maturity. Infertile couples could hire a "hyena" (another man) to impregnate the wife if the problem

Magical Powers

Claims of magical powers include the famous "lock-up" of women in Mangochi (see page 91) and "magical sex," in which men can have sexual activity with other women without any physical contact—a sort of Wi-Fi connection sex!

The Tumbuka people of Phoka are feared to have more magical powers than any other tribe. The Sena people are rumored to have the ability to create a "crocodile" even in a cup and swallow their enemies. In Karonga, they are accused of punishing their foes by removing bones from their flesh while alive. In Mulanje, as late as October 2017, rumors were rife of bloodsuckers that would turn into a dog or a cat after sucking one's blood. The fascinating stories of "Wi Fi" or "Blue tooth" sex to "locked" women all have one thing in common—no victim has ever come forward to confirm them.

was with the man. For the Ngoni, after the death of a wife, a man could be offered the young sister of the dead wife in a ritual called *skazi*.

Most these rituals have now been banned by traditional leaders and their communities, although reports still appear of people following the old customs in most rural areas. They have been accused of fueling the spread of HIV/AIDS and of early marriages for girls. A revised Wills and Inheritance Act has imposed a legal framework to protect widows and others from being abused in the name of culture.

chapter four

MAKING FRIENDS

FRIENDSHIP

For Malawians, friendship means spending a lot of time together and joining in with common activities. For men, sports, beer, and religion are the main after-work bonding activities. They are expected to leave home to the womenfolk and meet their friends outside—mainly for drinking sessions. Men rarely display emotion in public, so they don't exchange gifts or demonstrate closeness to other men. Women spend most leisure time together shopping or attending events in which they have a common interest.

There are no demands on friendship, save for giving one's time and helping if needed. Malawians are very friendly by nature, and it is easy for anyone, including foreigners, to integrate into local society, or to break into a circle of friendship, such as a beer-drinking crowd or a group that socializes outside home, just by joining in their conversation. Many foreigners have developed lifelong friendships with Malawians in this way, or by having met on a bus, at work, at church, or at a soccer match.

The principle is sharing—one should be open to sharing anything, from joining in a discussion other

people are having to answering questions about
oneself. Malawians love people who share their stories.
Most friends are open with each other, though for a
visitor it is important to take the cue from the hosts.
At pubs, where strangers become friends more quickly,
the one who buys the drinks is the friend of everyone.

For outsiders, an easy way of making friends in
Malawi is to be available for social events and to be
prepared to become part of the community. Social
activities may take place after a church service.
Normally, when visitors come to a new church,
they are introduced to the whole congregation, and
in most cases, local Church leaders will visit the
newcomers at home. Sometimes they may hold a
special prayer meeting at the house. Opening one's
house to such events will enable one to be absorbed
into the community quite quickly. Visitors should
expect and learn to enjoy the intrusive and private
questions that will be asked by their new friends for
them to be trusted as part of the group. Readiness to
help is essentially expected in cases where there is a

need, and being with people, visiting the sick, attending weddings, funerals, or other family events are all the best ways to guarantee one is a friend among Malawians. The extended family system in Malawi is such that it seems everyone is related to everyone else.

NICKNAMES FOR FOREIGNERS

Malawians are very good at identifying foreign nationals among them. Those whom they like are given clan names. Most volunteers have left Malawi with lifelong friendships and honorary titles. Though respect, the character of the individual, and admiration are the main reasons for giving a foreigner a name they can relate to easily, there are times when it has stemmed from a simple misunderstanding of the pronunciation of the foreigner's name. The name Sir Gregory has ended up as "Segelege"—indeed, a whole township has been called by this corrupted name. A family name in Mchinji was changed to "Camera" because their father used to carry a camera for a Catholic priest. Two brothers, John and Fredrick Moir, both bespectacled, were referred to by the locals as "those wearing glasses," and the Chewa word, *mandala*, stuck. Corrupted names included "Angelo Goveya," a mispronunciation of "Angels Go There," and "Naisi" in Zomba after white settlers used to describe the area as "very nice." A Canadian Catholic priest and anthropologist Father Claude Boucher has been given his local clan name, Chisale, added to his own name, for his work at Mua Mission in Dedza, where he runs the largest cultural museum in Malawi.

SOCIALIZING

The best place to meet Malawians is generally at a religious or social event, or for men simply at drinking places, which differ according to the type of people one wants to meet. For women, musical and Church events, and weddings are good places to meet and learn about each other. At work, the socializing will depend on the type of work: volunteers tend to get close to the communities they serve in, while in a formal work situation, most Malawians will not readily socialize with their bosses or expatriates. For people at that level, golf clubs and upscale bars would be better places to socialize. For men, alcohol at any level does the trick, particularly if you are buying. If you invite a Malawian to an event or for a drink, it means you are paying. In the West, if someone informally suggests you join them to go to a pub or a restaurant, you share the bill, whereas in Malawi the person who invites pays for everything. The more one buys, the more friends one acquires. Most Malawians will actually call you a brother or cousin, despite the visible skin color differences. Alternatively, go to a soccer match! You will find that soccer is the second religion for most Malawians at all social levels.

COMMUNAL LIVING

The more one joins in with the social activities of a community, the more integrated one can become. As we have seen, Malawi is a communal society. In rural areas communities share almost everything. People even share their time to help produce food, wash clothes, and brew traditional beer to raise money. Children are part of the community structure; they are expected to help the elderly and obey orders from everyone in the community.

Neighbors, even those in urban areas where they have no relations, will share their food with anybody seeking help. If a visitor shows up at a mealtime, they will be invited to eat, without fail.

TRANSACTIONAL SEX

Until the advent of social media, sex was treated as a private matter and restricted to adults. Prostitution, until the later 1990s, though illegal and remaining so, was restricted to bars and the like, and very few men would sit openly with a woman in a public place. Arrangements for a potential encounter were made in dark corners, and payment usually made in advance. Due to the growing number of young women drinking, it is now common for a woman to walk over to a man and ask him to buy her a drink. Caution should be exercised. Very drunk men have been robbed of their money and valuables when they have taken unknown women to their hotel rooms. It is worth asking bartenders whether the woman at the bar is well known to them.

Foreign women looking for Malawian men have no such problems. Most young men would relish a sexual encounter with a white woman, and would not demand anything in return; it would be regarded as an achievement for them. Along the lakeshore, it is common to see young white women in the arms of tour guides. Many have ended up falling in love and getting married.

The prevalence of HIV/AIDS has been dropping, but for transactional and casual sex it is vital to use condoms.

Good and Bad

There are historical tales of women at a fishing village in the lakeshore district of Mangochi who were famous for their perfect sex and love sessions. Legend has it that the women would, while naked, carry a naked man to the bathroom and bathe him. Many businessmen who went to buy fish for resale ended up staying permanently, or just blowing all their funds at this village. The myth persists, and yet nobody has confirmed this sexual practice.

From the same district, however, there are reports of the "magic lock," where husbands were able to lock their wives' private parts by magic—a useful trick for the men from this area, who often traveled to South Africa. If a man had sex with a married woman whose husband was away, he would be unable to remove himself from her. While scientifically there is proof of sexual locking being possible between a man and woman, there has been no confirmation of it in Mangochi. The myth includes the belief that the only way for the two to be unlocked is for them to confess to the husband.

Outside the low dives and hook-up joints, transactional sex is replaced by negotiation. Women will rarely have sex with someone who is not remotely connected to them. In these circumstances one would start a basic relationship and move on from there. Malawian women warmly welcome gifts, but it is not advisable, as anywhere else, to start a relationship with an engaged or married woman, though many do it, at great risk.

MIXED-RACE RELATIONSHIPS

Malawians are generally open to mixed-race marriages. Such a marriage would interest the whole village, and it would normally be necessary to hold a traditional wedding to keep the folks there happy. For a society that values children highly, it is important for the young people to visit the home village, that the in-laws, intrusive as it may be, be

allowed to come to town, and for the whole family to be lavished with hospitality and gifts. This applies to all ages. In-laws can make or unmake a marriage, and getting along with them is one of the most important secrets of a successful relationship with a Malawian.

LENDING MONEY AND OTHER ITEMS

A typical aspect of sharing is "borrowing." The perception that white people are rich, and have long been donors, means that Malawians rarely see the need to return loaned items. In most cases, if you lend something, you should not have any expectation of getting it back, so it's best not to lend anything you will regret not seeing again. The same applies to money. If a significant amount is involved, it would be prudent to find out the track record of the would-be borrower and make a judgment about whether or not to make the "loan."

CONVERSATIONS

The nature of conversations depends on age and place. The older the company, the more one is expected to show respect and greet everyone at the start. Conversations generally begin with the people you are next to, or near, and you will be expected to greet them and have a little chat with them. If you are a woman, a conversation will probably start with compliments—about anything from your clothes or your hair, to asking where you bought something. Questions are taken as a sign of interest, and nodding one's head and offering compliments along the way will be greatly appreciated. Men's talk will either be about sports—mainly soccer—or reactions to news and current affairs.

Conversations in pubs are more open, but most people are not comfortable discussing politics with strangers. The best thing is to take the cue from the conversation, laugh along, and share comparisons from your country. There are generally no "no-go" subjects, though one should be reticent about discussing women's bodies or sex. The conversations will center mainly on how people live or view various issues.

INVITATIONS HOME

Neighbors don't ordinarily expect special written invitations to events. Most invitations will be verbal notice for a party, an upcoming wedding or engagement, or a special ceremony. Your hosts will expect you to contribute to and actively participate in the party. Timing is of no consequence—as long as one turns up, everyone is happy. Parties are expected to last the whole night. Barbecues, with lots of meat—mainly beef or pork, chicken, boiled cow's feet and "hard chicken" (a local breed)—are popular for home parties. At some parties you might be requested to bring some food and beer, and at others you'll bring your own drink and the hosts will provide the food.

In the villages, parties can be visits of one village team to another, which might last the whole weekend, while weddings, engagements, and the installation of chiefs are some of the biggest events you are expected to attend and to contribute something to, whether a live animal, food, or money. In most cases, dress is left to the guests to decide, save for urban parties, which are either themed or have a dress code specified by the hosts.

If you want to visit someone at home, these days you are expected to call in advance, not just show up. However, if you happen to meet someone while you are out, and start to chat, it might end up in sharing lunch or dinner. People are encouraged to conduct reciprocal visits. Always comment on the attractiveness of the house and the deliciousness of the food. When there are leftovers your host will encourage you to take some home, if you have praised them highly.

The conversations are normally informal, though women will be expected to talk with other women and men with other men. In a visit to someone's home, female guests are generally expected to go into the kitchen and help, though if you are foreigner you can be excused—but you can still go into the kitchen and chat, even if they don't let you help.

Don't arrive too early. It's best to arrive from five to ten minutes before the set time if visiting a new friend. Ordinarily you can call if you are running late, and it will be acceptable. It is customary for visitors to bring a gift, and for the hosts to offer one to the visitor when leaving their home.

Each household will have its own etiquette in eating or sitting at a table— wait for your hosts to advise. After the meal, you are expected to retreat to another room for a long conversation. It is acceptable to stay for an hour after eating, but if you are in a group, wait for one of the locals to bid farewell first before you leave. A thank-you note is not necessary, though on your arrival home you can call to report that you have had a safe trip and thank the hosts for their hospitality.

chapter five

THE MALAWIANS AT HOME

HOUSING

Most Malawians live in rural areas, where the home is typically a mud hut with a thatched roof. An ordinary household will consist of a main house, usually with three bedrooms—one for the parents, one for the male children, and one for the female children. In the villages the kitchen and bathroom will be outside the house. The youngsters are expected to leave their parents' home when they reach puberty, the girls from different families going to live in an all-girls' one-roomed house within the village called a *gowelo*, and boys going to live in an *mphala*. Each hut is "painted" with colorful red, gray, or black soils, using the beauty of the local habitat. Each family has a kitchen, and the children in the *gowelo* and *mphala,* though they are

supported, are expected to have a small garden and fend for themselves.

Though this lifestyle has changed considerably, with education being a priority for most children today, many of the young people now remain with their parents, and most will only leave years later, after they have started work.

It is common now to find homes with baked-brick walls and corrugated iron roofs. These houses may be small for an average Malawian family of five, but ownership brings a sense of pride. It is always advisable to compliment people on how good their home and its surrounding areas look.

Malawi's towns were well planned under one-party rule, with stringent law enforcement ensuring law and order and housing units being allocated in designated places. Population pressure, urban migration, and new freedoms have seen the cities swell and people now construct anything anywhere. Housing units remain graded as townships, although many of them are slums.

Because of demand due to the growing land shortage, many families on the outskirts of major cities have sold their land and moved farther away, and the result could be an imposing mansion next to a village—all happily living side by side.

THE HOUSEHOLD

A Malawian family today has an average of two to three children, though until 1985 most would have as many as five, and a decade before that it could have been anything up to twelve. Children are regarded as wealth, and childbearing as a very important function. Childbirth is one of the many family events that, once you have been informed, you need to acknowledge right away with a brief visit or some form of congratulations.

In a typical village household, the family is a close-knit unit, usually augmented by cousins and other

extended family members. In most cases, relatives, both distant and close, come to live in the house for some time for various reasons. Well-to-do families support their poor relations, enabling them to go to school, helping with finances generally, and in other ways. Though in urban areas most people live with their children only, resident relations are a common feature, and it shows that a person is of good character if he has many visitors in his household. Life in both town and village is communal, where people eat meals together and sometimes, due to lack of space, even share sleeping areas. Guests are normally allocated a child's bedroom.

Not in Front of the Children

In Malawi adults are expected to be pillars of society and good role models for the young. Parents should never quarrel in front of children. Visitors to a family are expected to be cheerful, and to play with the children of the house for much of the time. Children, as elsewhere, are inquisitive and persistent and it is seen as culturally insensitive to ignore a child who is trying to engage a visitor's attention.

Talk about sexual matters, shouting, and profanity are not allowed in the presence of children, and if one is angry one should remember that boiling rage or bad language can result in a summons to the chief's court if someone complains. Drunkards have landed themselves in trouble for showing up after a beer session and singing or shouting inappropriate words in front of children; when they are sober elders will normally visit them to rebuke them.

DEMOGRAPHY

Malawi is a youthful nation, densely populated, and with one of the highest fertility rates. The annual population growth is around 3 percent, and 60 percent of its population are below the age of thirty-five. Rapid population growth has led to widespread environmental degradation, dwindling land for food production, and increased rural–urban migration, leading the city slums to swell, and many people remain unemployed. The population was estimated to have hit 18 million in 2016.

The country has remained dependent on tobacco, which accounts for at least 60 percent of its exports and foreign exchange earnings. The conditions of the intense labor system on the tobacco estates, known as "tenancy," have been blamed for exacerbating poverty, and the low prices offered by the major tobacco companies have also sent many smallholder farmers into a cycle of debt and poverty. The country's youthful population presents an opportunity for growth, if the dependence on agriculture can be minimized and investments made in other sectors as well.

Population control and abortion remain culturally, politically, and religiously sensitive, and influential religious leaders keep mobilizing people to demonstrate against abortion and same-sex relationships. Thousands each year are treated for post-abortion care after attempting to terminate pregnancies unsafely.

Though literacy has gone up, and though urbanites have now reduced the average number of children in a family to two or three, the emphasis on the family as a childbearing institution is likely to continue for the next generation. The education sector will need to incorporate serious messages on population control, environmental management, and the impact of population growth to halt this trend.

CHILDBEARING AS A COMMUNITY CONCERN
If, after marriage, a year passes without the wife becoming pregnant, elders from both families will visit the couple. The women will ask the wife if everything is all right, and whether the man can perform. The men will ask the husband if he is enjoying his conjugal rights. Both are encouraged to try hard, as gossipers are watching. The thought of such pressure to come means that most young couples do in fact start a family within the first year of marriage. And if, after the birth of a first child, the pair decides to wait for more than three years, the elders will come and put on a show of playing with the child, and declare that he or she needs a playmate. Such intrusion always takes place in villages where every excuse—from needing to redress a balance by having a boy or a girl, to simply needing to have more children to support the parents in old age—is used to ensure that they do their duty to multiply.

WHO EARNS WHAT?
The formal employment sector is very small in Malawi, with the public service as the largest employer, hovering around 170,000 employees. The average salary in public service is the equivalent of US $70

per month, while the minimum wage is only US $30, which the majority of unskilled laborers take home.

Malawi is ranked the eighteenth-least developed country by the United Nations, with almost 40 percent living in extreme poverty, below the threshold of US $1 a day. Many are farmers and rely heavily on government subsidies to produce enough crops for their own food and the sale of surplus to cover other basic needs.

In rural areas, the absence of meaningful economic activity means dire poverty, sometimes no food, cutting down trees to eke a living out of selling firewood, and in many cases migration. Natural disasters such as floods and dry spells, exacerbated by climate change, affect the poorest families. Harvests fail, sending more into poverty.

There is a huge gap between low and high earners. The same is true in politics, where politicians in parliament are highly paid and have access to duty-free vehicles and concessional loans subsidized by the taxpayer.

A SENSE OF STYLE

Malawi's mixture of cultures and the strict dress code under three decades of dictatorship left a nation searching for an identity. For men and women, Sunday best is typically formal Western dress, and for the young, jeans and the latest trends in South Africa and America are always seen in the urban centers.

Local designers, such as Nzika Wear, have revolutionized fashions for men, who now sport the printed shirts that have become Friday wear in public offices after the government launched the Buy Malawian campaign in 2016. The urban centers continue to see a more American style, with trendy suits becoming fashionable in most nightclubs.

Moslems and some specific Churches, such as the Salvation Army, Apostolic Faith, Latter Day Saints, and Zion, have their own forms of dress, with the Zion being the most colorful. The growing number of Pentecostal movements have their own defined dressing styles, which include shiny and multicolored suits.

Women have largely stayed with the traditional *chitenje*, a long cloth that can be used as both formal and informal wear. It has different roles, and can be made into a blouse, skirt, scarf, headgear, or baby carrier.

THE DAILY ROUND

Most people are engaged in subsistence farming, and the day starts with the whole family, including the older children, rising around 4:00 a.m. and heading to work in the field. The mothers come back early to prepare breakfast, which usually consists of *nsima*, or maize flour porridge—with, for the lucky ones, some sugar or salt.

During a lean time of year, lunch is either skipped or takes the form of whatever can be found in the way of seasonal alternatives, such as mangoes, pumpkins, or sweet potatoes. The evening meal is normally huge, and is when the whole family will eat together. Only 15 percent of Malawians have access to electricity, meaning that in the majority of rural  areas many go to bed before 8:00 p.m.—leading to the joke that long nights are to blame for the rapid rise in population.

In urban areas, the many laborers in manufacturing and processing plants start their day early, walking to their places of work. Others, especially women, engage in trading in all sorts of food and products.

The markets in the urban centers start around 4:00 a.m., when trucks loaded with produce arrive in designated areas, and the traders buy wholesale. All kinds of food are available, from tomatoes to fresh fish. The traders then open the markets at around 6:00 a.m. and continue until 6:00 p.m. Visitors to Malawi find the open-air markets are the best places to get bargains.

For these market traders, breakfast is a rare treat, and their normally busy mornings mean their first

meal is at lunchtime. Some enterprising groups have opened food stalls and restaurants to suit all budgets.

So for those families, too, the real and main meal at home is dinner. The increase in television and radio broadcasting has encouraged families to acquire radios, which are a primary source of entertainment and news (it is estimated that 49 percent of the population own a radio).

In well-to-do households, satellite and local TV stations dominate their evening entertainment, while in rural areas people flock to the local trading places, where there are late markets, video showrooms, and places where they can just meet up with their friends. In such places a typical day would last as long as they can stretch it, since many households, as we have seen, don't have light.

GROWING UP IN MALAWI

Malawian children grow up in a culturally and religiously sensitive society. They are expected to respect their elders, contribute to household chores, go to school, play, and return home at a decent time. Girls growing up have a much tougher routine than boys, being taught how to keep the household clean at an early age.

With most of the population living in rural areas, life is generally tough, as poverty, hunger, and the lack of facilities affect many children's growth. Infant and child mortality is high, though it is currently falling owing to interventions and increased awareness. However, malnutrition and undernourishment remain high in all age groups.

Poverty is evident—most children cannot afford uniforms, proper shoes or, for young girls reaching puberty, even sanitary pads. School facilities are mainly poor in rural areas, so that in some cases the lack of decent classrooms and toilets for girls has seen a large number of girls leave school early.

In many rural areas girls have been denied educational opportunities and at times forced to get married and have children so that their families can collect a dowry or financial support from the husband. Such marriages have often turned abusive, with the women then bearing more children in the hope that their husbands will love them more.

Poverty, too, has led some boys to engage in petty crime. Many youths have migrated to South Africa or moved to the cities to trade as street vendors, as there is no proper social support structure, and there is pressure on children to help their families financially.

In urban areas, the majority of parents work, which means that children spend more time in school. There are limited recreational facilities around schools and in cities, and children have to invent their own games and find their own places to play to pass the idle hour.

The unique distinction of having a tough childhood has sometimes been a good factor. Most of the children who go to school work hard, as they realize that education is their only way out. There are incredible stories of orphans, goatherds, teen mothers, and the like, who have worked their way up from tough childhoods to become great men and women in Malawian society.

The greatest virtue of Malawian society is that it imparts knowledge and wisdom, survival skills, and a spirit of community sharing to the child. This is evident when people fall sick or grow old—children, not even from their immediate families, help to take care of everyone within the community.

EDUCATION

The Malawian education system is a hybrid born of the experiments of Kamuzu Banda and his successors. Schooling is modeled on the British education system, although local adaptation and the hurried implementation of free primary education after multiparty democracy returned in 1994 saw the plummeting of standards and quality control.

The country now runs on three parallel education systems, especially at the secondary and tertiary levels. Primary education in both public and Christian schools is for eight years, though many private schools complete the curriculum in six or seven years. In

standard eight, children sit for their Primary School
Leaving Certificate, which was enough in the 1980s
to get a job with the police or the now defunct Malawi
Young Pioneers, the paramilitary youth movement
under Kamuzu Banda. Those with good grades
are selected to go on to secondary school

Secondary education is for four years, after which
children sit for the Malawi School Certificate of
Education (MSCE), which is equivalent to the UK's
General Certificate of Secondary Education. Private
high schools offer GCE and A (Advanced) levels,
which means that a child can spend five to six years
in a private secondary school as opposed to four in
a public secondary school.

The first year in Malawi's state universities is
equivalent to Britain's A levels, so a degree program
is at least four years compared to the UK's three
on average. The quality of university education is
generally good, especially at the College of Medicine

and Kamuzu College of Nursing. The Law and Education faculties at Chancellor College are rated highly. The University of Mzuzu, a second state university, opened in late 2000; the Lilongwe University of Agriculture and Natural Resources came after the merging of Bunda College, Natural Resources College, and Mwimba Agricuture Institute in 2010; and the newly built Chinese funded Malawi University of Science and Technology opened in 2014. The four state universities are expected to grow alongside four new planned universities.

English is widely spoken in Malawi, and the literacy rate has gone up to 65 percent of the population.

KAMUZU ACADEMY

This grammar school was built as the personal education project of Kamuzu Banda. Until his death in 1997, only white people were allowed to teach. The Academy is called the "Eton of Africa," and follows a strict British curriculum. Two students from each of the then twenty-four districts were offered scholarships, which allowed poor children to gain access to a world-class education. The scholarships were stopped by the Bakili Muluzi administration, but later resumed by Bingu wa Mutharika. Many teachers now are black Africans, though a black man or woman has yet to head the exclusive educational institution. Many African presidents used to send their children to the Academy.

chapter six

TIME OUT

LEISURE

Malawians, hardworking as they are, make sure they have plenty of leisure time too. Most of their spare time is spent with groups of friends in idle talk, sharing a drink, and sometimes playing a board game called *bawo*. Even as early as 7:00 a.m. some pubs are open and people are drinking—especially in the townships. Social media Web sites such as  Facebook have revealed how much Malawians, even during working hours, are posting and commenting online.

How much leisure people have depends on their age and the day of the week. The young tend to have spare time and fun every day, while the adults relax mainly on weekends. In recent times adults have been encroaching on young people's territory, with many drinking alongside them, playing soccer, and even going to festivals that used to be patronized only by the young.

During the week, leisure time for people in the villages generally comes after finishing the day's work on the farm. During the farming season, the men return to check the fields around 4:00 p.m. and if they have vegetable gardens they water them. After the harvest is taken in nobody goes back to work. Usually people relax and start to enjoy some leisure after lunch, and this is the time for visiting.

Men congregate in the shade of the huge trees, sipping traditional brews; those with money to spare may go to bottle stores or taverns. Bottle stores will normally sell bottled branded beer, and taverns sell traditional beers, which can be the commercial Chibuku, or cheap equivalents. Adults are more likely to frequent taverns in rural and suburban areas.

For young men, soccer, known as "football," is the main leisure activity, apart from drinking. Soccer in Malawi is second to religion, and hours are spent either discussing the game or playing it. Visitors with a knowledge of soccer find it easy to make friends, and even easier if they can play. Social soccer has been growing across the country, and working people play on the weekends—most of the games eventually turning into drinking sessions.

For women and girls also, leisure time is spent primarily in groups. Women have only limited social time between their household chores. Mostly they attend church and community activities, and girls at school play netball—an early British adaptation of basketball—at which Malawi has ranked number one in Africa and is among the top five global teams. Some chores allow women to spend hours together, chatting and exchanging tips on life experiences as they work. These are very important moments of relaxation for women, as they generally work very long hours. In urban areas, while women meet in social circles, midweek is usually reserved for family times and looking after the children.

It's usually quite quiet from Monday to Wednesday, and then the men start going out after 7:00 p.m. to congregate, usually at drinking places, to watch soccer, especially the English Premier League, which has a huge following.

Weekends are the main leisure times for most Malawians. Men usually focus on social soccer and then continuous drinking, which often ends on Sunday night. Women tend to have long social programs that may include charity work, visiting hospitals, weddings, church engagements, and other group activities that may take them away from home for hours.

A recent phenomenon, especially among those with disposable incomes, is to drive out of town to newly developed spots such as game parks, Lake Malawi's beaches, and tea plantations. This local tourism sector is growing so rapidly that almost every public holiday has a corresponding festival, usually along the lake.

EATING OUT

Malawi has all kinds of food, but the main dish across the country is *nsima*, made from maize, cassava, or millet flour—a thick, hardened porridge (known

as "grits" in the US and *ugali* in Swahili). The most commonly available type found in almost all food stalls and restaurants is the one made from maize (corn) flour. The other *nsima* is made from cassava flour and is dominant along the lakeshore. The *nsima* meal is commonly accompanied by beef, chicken, or fish. The national dish is usually *nsima* with *chambo*—a tilapia fish found in Lake Malawi, normally grilled on a charcoal burner. *Chambo* is tasty with chips (fries) and salads, or with rice. *Kilombero*, the special rice grown in Malawi, has a good flavor. Rice is the staple food along the growing areas. Potatoes, both sweet and normal, make up other main dishes for Malawians.

Menus are therefore dominated by a choice of *nsima*, rice, or chips, with corresponding accompaniments of beef, chicken, or fish. Food is traditionally eaten with the fingers.

The growth of a multinational society in the urban areas means that all global cuisines are readily available,

TIPPING

Tipping is the norm, but there is no pressure to tip. It's better to tip little and often, and to make sure that everyone involved in the service you have received gets something.

In a restaurant, tip 5–10 percent of the bill. Hotels and lodges may suggest leaving a collective tip of US $5 per guest per night when checking out to be distributed among the staff.

A suitable tip for a porter or a local guide for a one-off service is anything from 100 to 500 kwacha. For a private tour, the main guide expects between US $50 and $100 per guest, and the driver around US $20.

with Chinese, Italian, British, and American foods being dominant. South African and Tanzanian dishes are also common, and with the influx of

Nigerians, West African meals are found in cities such as Lilongwe.

NIGHTLIFE
Save for pubs, most of which open from Monday to Sunday, nightlife in Malawi really starts from Wednesdays, depending on the location. The top bars and clubs usually open from Tuesdays, but they come alive from Wednesdays, when they offer a variety of themes. Most Wednesdays are "rhumba nights"—mainly playing old African music; Thursdays are ladies' nights; and on Fridays and Saturdays the clubs are packed to overflowing. On Sunday afternoons there are live band performances known as "jazz afternoons," after the long-standing Sunday jazz performances by Malawian artists at the then Lingadzi Inn Gardens, which briefly moved to the Capital City Motel. On Sundays, most clubs with gardens or space will host jazz afternoons.

There are new and trendy upscale places with an international atmosphere, and there are others that offer a traditional Malawian ambience, such as Kumbali Lodge, famous for hosting Madonna during her now frequent trips to Malawi.

There are quiet, laid-back places that offer pleasant surroundings for rendezvous, and there many romantic nightspots outside the city—perfect for honeymooners and those wanting to renew their love lives.

Most clubs have a dress code. Most require you to pay cash before you get your drink, and only major hotels and clubs have electronic machines for payments by card.

Other 24/7 areas are near bus terminals, or major markets, or small towns where trucks park. The pubs around these are various low-budget bars and meeting places for transactional sex. Though classified as high-risk for HIV/AIDS, most of these pubs offer an insight into the fun enjoyed by ordinary people. If you do visit such a place, your personal security should be a priority, and you should go with a trusted guide.

In the main cities there are crowded local joints—Basiyawo in Zomba; Grill at Chirimba; Kamba and Chinseu in Blantyre; and Biwi, Devil Street, and Bwandilo in Lilongwe, which operate in populous locations and where the fun is unlimited. They are usually safe for a traveler, and taxis are available all night.

SPORTS

Soccer, as we have seen, is Malawi's second religion. Soccer grounds are prominent features along all the

country or intercity roads, and on weekends they are filled with competitive games. The Malawi National Football Team is called "Flames"—a literal translation of the name Malawi.

The biggest local soccer clubs are the Mighty Wanderers and the Big Bullets—they sometimes add sponsors' names to their own names—and their rivalry is infectious. Their supporters create a carnival atmosphere and any major win is greeted with street jubilation and weeks of long soccer commentary.

The English Premier League has fanatical followers in Malawi, and on most game nights the pubs are full, with lively outbursts of joy or despair whenever a team scores or misses an opportunity. Violence is rare, but it's wise to remember which team one supports, to avoid being in the wrong crowd!

Basketball and volleyball, though they used to be much played, are now mainly college and beach games respectively. Beach soccer is becoming popular, owing to the large social soccer groups that travel to the lake.

Pool is played among drinkers, and has slowly killed darts, which used to be the number one sport in pubs. Successful middle-class businessmen are taking up golf, while karate and bodybuilding are becoming all the rage even in the local townships.

Almost every kind of sport is available in Malawi, and it is very likely that people will follow any new game that is introduced, until either they are tired of it or they simply become too busy with their first love—soccer.

Malawian women have dominated netball, with the national team breaking into the top three of global rankings and remaining a major powerhouse in Africa. Interestingly a male coach, Griffin Saenda, is credited with the phenomenal rise in ranking of the netball team christened "The Queens."

THE ARTS

The art "industry" in Malawi is limited to painting, television, and stage drama, which sadly is dying.

There are art galleries in Lilongwe, Blantyre, and some tourist spots. Museums include the Chichiri Museum, which has a well-documented history covering the era of David Livingstone, the Arab slave traders, and the various transitions of Malawi. The Cultural and Museum Centre in Karonga is another great place for visitors, as are the Chamale Museum at Mua in Dedza, with its great woodcarvings and cultural activities; the Lake Museum in Mangochi; the Postal Museum at Nyungwe; and the Mission museum at Livingstonia, in Rumphi. Live performances, mainly of music, are always put on during weekends, and are an essential part of the Malawi experience.

CURRENCY AND BANKING

The country has Visa and MasterCard ATMs and points of sale, mainly in the urban areas. Travelers' checks can be cashed in most tourist cities and towns. Banking facilities are available in all the major cities and towns, operating from 8:00 a.m. to 3:00 p.m. or 4:00 p.m. Mondays to Fridays; some open on Saturdays.

MUST-SEE TOURIST ATTRACTIONS

Malawi's mountains, plantations, lakes, and rivers offer a remarkable array of activities for visitors. A game safari, hiking and walking, and a beach holiday are all within a short distance of each other, so no time is lost in traveling. Owing to its small size, even a ten- to

fourteen-day vacation will allow a visitor to explore the full length of the country. It is best to do this by the three administrative regions: Northern, Central, and Southern Malawi.

Northern Malawi
Nyika National Park. Small chartered flights can take you to the Nyika National Park, the largest in Malawi. It extends across Nyika Plateau, a granitic dome about 7,875 feet (2,400 m) above sea level, and is great for

trekking and mountain biking. The landscape is rich in wild flowers, and has more than 150 types of orchid during the rainy season. Large herds of antelope, roan, eland, and duiker are found almost everywhere in the park. Zebras and leopards are very common on the plateau, which is one of the largest on the continent. Jackals, elephants, and buffalo can be seen there too. There are more than four hundred bird species, including the rare Denham's bustard and the wattled crane. The great waterfalls, pools, and a lake make the park a honeymooners' paradise.

Vwaza Marsh Wildlife Reserve. From Nyika, almost next door is the Vwaza Marsh Wildlife Reserve. Starting from Hewe, all the way to Kazuni, it offers a great bush game experience, with its vegetation of forests, woodland, and marsh. It has a great variety of birds, large herds of elephants and hippos, antelope, baboons, and buffalo. Lake Kazuni, one of the five Malawian lakes, is located on the marsh.

The Livingstonia Mission, named after David Livingstone, at Golodi, at a height of about 3,000 feet (900 m), is a historical settlement of the first missionaries to Malawi. It has a church museum, Mantchewe Falls, and fascinating bridges. Other Church missions worth exploring include Embangweni and Ekwendeni.

Karonga has a cultural museum; its rich contribution to Africa's beginnings include remains of the Malawisaurus dinosaur and some of the oldest human remains. It was a center for the slave trade in the nineteenth century.

Nkhata Bay is the "Caribbean" of Malawi, and is the part of the lake with the deepest waters for scuba diving, as well as beautiful sandy beaches.

Kande, Makuzi, and ***Chintheche***, including the boma (the main district administrative center), where there is a port, offer exciting experiences of lakeshore life in Malawi.

Viphya Plantation, one of the largest plantations in Africa, has a variety of sights and activities, from climbing Elephant Rock to lodging, trekking, and birdwatching. The forest is rich with wild fruits, mushrooms, and other delicacies. Leopards and baboons can be spotted in the dense forest.

Likoma Island is on Lake Malawi, but in Mozambican waters. It's a perfect place to wind up after a cruise from Nkhatabay, Chipoka, or Monkey Bay on the aging *Illala* or newly built *Chilembwe* vessels. The grand edifice of the hundred-year-old cathedral, with its stained glass and carved soapstone, is a landmark on the main island of Likoma. On Saturdays there are cultural activities, held jointly with Mozambican communities, that include traditional dance competitions.

Chizumulu is another, smaller, fishing island.

All the islands have great beaches, and a music festival takes place every summer.

Central Malawi

The country's major airport, Kamuzu International, is in Lilongwe, the capital, which makes it convenient for anyone trying to explore the whole of Malawi. The region has two wildlife parks.

Kasungu National Park, once a home to all sorts of wildlife, still has animals but is suffering from intense poaching due to its long boundary with Zambia. Kasungu was home to Malawi's first president, Hastings Kamuzu Banda, who built the elitist Kamuzu Academy on the site of his first classroom under a baobab tree at Mtunthama, near his father's village.

Nkhotakota Wildlife Reserve is home to two thousand species of animals, including five hundred elephants that were relocated from the southern parks in 2016 and 2017. The reserve has great vegetative and natural cover and rivers good for angling. Nkhotakota also has hot springs, a pottery

workshop, a mission site, sugar plantations, and the old mosque of Jumbe, a Swahili Arab trader.

Ntchisi Forest Reserve, one of Africa's last remaining rainforests, has interesting orchids, birds, and samango monkeys. The reserve is popular for hiking and is known for its picturesque surroundings.

Salima offers some of the finest beaches along Lake Malawi, at Senga Bay and Chipoka. It is home to the Kuti Game Ranch, and there are numerous bird islands on the lake. The Sand Festival is one of the biggest events, hosted by the Sunbird Livingstonia Hotel. On the drive from Chipoka, in Salima, to Mangochi or Dedza, is the Mua Mission of the Catholic Order of the White Fathers, with the large

collection of Nyau masks at the Chamaere Musuem, which is part of the Ku Ngoni Art Centre.

Going up the steep and winding Khwekherere road are lake views, with small waterfalls adding to the beauty. Dedza, a thriving border town, and the highest town in Malawi, has a famous pottery workshop, and nearby forests covering Stone Age and early rock paintings—a UNESCO world heritage site, which should not be missed.

Lilongwe, the capital, offers a view of a developing Malawi. The city center, with its vegetative cover, has the State House, the government seat named Capital Hill, the Parliament, the Mausoleum of Kamuzu Banda, the Bingu National Stadium, and colonial Lilongwe's old town, which contains some historical buildings, markets, and colorful mosques. The city's water source, the Kamuzu Dam, is on the way to Dzalanyama Forest Reserve, a woodland area that used to stock a variety of animals.

The Lilongwe Wildlife Centre, located at the Lilongwe Nature Sanctuary right in the city center,

offers an interesting experience for business travelers who haven't the time to go to the parks. The center is the only emergency clinic and hospital for wildlife animals and for anti-poaching advocacy, and provides a rare conservation service for the whole continent.

Southern Malawi
This region is the most developed, and it has major attractions. The Shire River, which is the major outlet for Lake Malawi, passes through most of the districts all the way to the Zambezi River. The Shire has the Nkula and Kapichira Falls, which are main source of Malawi's electricity.

Lake Malawi National Park at Cape Maclear is a World Heritage Site, with more than five hundred species of fish found nowhere else in the world. It offers some of the best lakeshore activities in Malawi, from the fish that eat from your hand, to kayaking, sailing, and scuba diving, and simple enjoyment of one of the best-kept beaches in the world. The SS *Gwendolen*, a British steamship on the lake, fought the

first naval action of the First World War against the German steamship *Hermann von Wissman*.

A drive from Mangochi toward Zomba offers the experience of a Malawian village and religious life, with Catholic and Islamic structures facing each other. At Balaka, one of Malawi's largest churches in Vatican colors dominates the landscape, while on the Liwonde River there are cruises into the Liwonde National Park.

Liwonde National Park is one of the few parks that offer boat safaris, walking safaris tracking rhino, and truck safaris. Huge numbers of elephants, crocodiles, and hippos can be seen in or around the river, and birds, kudu, bushbuck, and sable are abundant. The black rhino was reintroduced some years ago, and there are lions and leopards.

Zomba is the old colonial capital at the base of Zomba Plateau. There is a historical war memorial, and colonial administrative buildings. A good road takes you up to the plateau, around 6,000 feet (1,800 m)

above sea level. Chingwe Hall, Emperor's View, a trout farm, and Mulunguzi Dam, all on the top of the plateau, and the Kuchawe Inn, a hotel, all add to the best experiences of Zomba. A drive from Zomba can take you via the Postal Museum at Nyungwe into Chiradzulu, which was home to the first uprising against colonialism led by national hero John Chilembwe in 1915, and now has coffee plantations.

Thyolo has some of the most beautiful scenery in the world, dominated by tea plantations, and includes the Zoa Falls. The newly constructed Malawi University of Science and Technology is here. The plantations continue into Mulanje, where an island seems to emerge in the sky: Mulanje

Mountain, a massif with beautiful peaks, waterfalls, and natural dams. The highest peak is Sapitwa, about 9,850 feet (3,000 m) above sea level, making it the highest in Southern Africa.

Blantyre (named after David Livingstone's
birthplace) is the commercial capital of the country,
with most of Malawi's industries, and modern
buildings mixed in with historical ones, such as the
Mandala House, which now houses archives and
a library. Blantyre has two major towns: Blantyre
and Limbe. Limbe is a trading place, and has some
colonial buildings, while on the connecting highway
there are landmarks such as the Independence
Arch, a university, a major hospital, and an old
clock tower. A national museum is located along
the highway. A thriving arts and crafts market exists
right in the city center. The Victorian church of
St. Michael and All Angels, on the way to Chileka
Airport, reflects the English influence on Blantyre.

A forty-five-minute trip south takes you down
to the Shire Valley. The descent, down the side of a
steep hill, gives one a view of the meandering Shire
River, natural lagoons, and sugar plantations.

The Majete Wildlife Reserve has the "Big Five," and now boasts the highest population of wildlife. The reserve has beautiful riverbanks and offers safaris, bush walks, and accommodation.

The Lengwe National Park has beautiful Nyala antelopes.

The Mwabvi Wildlife Reserve is a community-oriented reserve, famous for its Elephant Marsh, and is a heaven for birdwatchers.

The remote district of Nsanje offers a trip into Mozambique by boat to see where the Shire River meets the Zambezi, and, for anthropologists, the Mbona shrine at Khulubvi—a very important shrine of the Mang'anja people.

chapter seven

TRAVEL, HEALTH, & SAFETY

All of Malawi's twenty-eight districts, save for Likoma Island, are connected by hard-surfaced roads, and these major intercity roads are generally in good condition. Most of the connecting minor roads are passable, even in the rainy season.

ARRIVING

There are three international airports in Malawi. The main one is Kamuzu International Airport, which has daily flights between Lilongwe and Johannesburg, Nairobi, and Addis Ababa, and direct flights to Lusaka, Harare, and Dar es Salaam. The second airport is Chileka, which has direct flights to Nairobi, Addis Ababa, and Johannesburg. Regional links between Malawi and Kenya, South Africa, Tanzania, Zambia, and Zimbabwe are provided by Malawian Airlines and some of the national airlines of those countries. Such connections can sometimes be used in conjunction with another African or European airline flying from Europe to these countries. Malawian Airlines, partly owned

by Ethiopian Airlines, offers connections around
the world. Malawi-based air charter companies link
Malawi to its neighbors. The small new international
airport on Likoma Island mainly handles charter
flights.

Visas can be obtained at the port of entry for
US $75.00 for visitors from the US and most of
the European Union countries. Other countries
require a visa to be obtained at a Malawi embassy
or consulate.

There are direct buses between Lilongwe and
Dar es Salaam, Lusaka, Harare, and Johannesburg,
and buses from Mzuzu, Mzimba, and Blantyre to
Harare and Johannesburg.

There are road, rail, and/or water routes into
Malawi from Tanzania, Zambia, and Mozambique.
You should assume that the border posts close from
about 6:00 p.m. and reopen at 7:00 a.m. Visitors
requiring a visa may find it difficult to obtain one
at border posts, and are advised to get it in advance.

It is also advisable, if you have a vehicle, to check the documentation requirements before traveling. The current requirements for a vehicle to enter Malawi are: third-party insurance, obtainable at the border; a temporary import permit, also obtainable at the border; and the vehicle's registration certificate—if the vehicle is not owned by the driver, a letter of authorization from the owner or car rental company is also required.

INTERCITY CONNECTIONS

There are daily flights between the two major cities of Lilongwe and Blantyre. There is an executive coach service between the three cities of Blantyre, Lilongwe, and Mzuzu. These coaches have special bus stations, mainly at hotels and other designated places, and they don't stop along the route. They are normally the only peaceful means of road transportation.

Traveling on ordinary buses can, however, be fun for first timers. It's a lively experience, with a generally noisy atmosphere. There's music, sometimes a TV, dominated by Nigerian movies, and a constant buzz of everyone talking to everyone else. Passengers buy and try all sorts of snacks, from roasted corn cobs to boiled eggs and locally fried chips, and urge each other to try them too. You are likely to be offered a share. It's best to refuse politely, as accepting might well create the expectation that next time it will be your turn to buy and share. In minibuses, the situation includes your expected participation in ongoing conversations, which could range from soccer to politics or other current affairs.

Sometimes an entertaining conductor can make a journey amusing, with his calls at stops to attract more passengers on board.

"Any Droppings?"

Many of the minibus conductors have not completed school, and on one journey a young conductor wanted to impress a group of ladies in his bus by speaking English. Before every stop he would call out, "Any droppings at the next stage?"

Ordinary buses and minibuses depart almost every minute from the Wenela bus depot, the Lilongwe bus depot, and the Mzuzu bus depot. The buses travel to nearly all districts, and are mainly complemented by minibuses. The minibuses go faster, even though they are always overloaded, but their safety record is poor, so it's advisable to use the big buses for long-distance journeys. These are anyway recommended for additional sightseeing trips.

Generally, Malawi's size and the road conditions make travel from one end of the country to the other easy. All the major wildlife reserves, lakeshore districts, and other places are accessible by the all-weather paved roads. The gravel and unsurfaced roads in rural areas are generally adequate, though caution should be exercised, and local knowledge of the area would be helpful in bad weather to avoid getting stuck in the mud. Rains are generally short, with the longest period recorded so far being about four and a half hours. Climate change, however, is bringing flash floods and landslides, and it is important at all times to check the road conditions before traveling.

GETTING AROUND TOWN

Malawi's urban planning generally separates residential buildings from the city centers. Hotels are the only residences located in the central areas, and one can walk around town on foot from most of them. Traveling on public transportation is generally safe, and minibuses are fine for short journeys in town. They are the major form of commuting into the cities from outside. They are cheap to use, and fares are collected by the conductor. People pack themselves in, beyond the number the regulations stipulate, and nobody is expected to complain about the crush. In the rural areas, transportation can be varied—from pickup trucks to ox carts, depending on location and the traveler's level of desperation.

Cycling is emerging as an alternative, with new companies registering to rent out bikes to visitors.

Taxis are available at all hotels, though they are generally expensive. Most of the big hotels also offer transportation to and from the airport.

DRIVING

Most international drivers' licenses are accepted in
Malawi. Driving is on the left, as in the UK. The
major roads make is possible for visitors to drive
safely around the country, but the narrower roads
are basically single lanes. Accidents are common
during festivals and the rainy season, and the best
plan may be to hire a local driver with the necessary
knowledge and experience.

Though most drivers on the road have licenses,
they may not have passed proper road tests, owing
to years of corruption at the road traffic department;
this has now been stopped through radical reforms.

The average speed limit in urban areas is
30 kmph (equivalent to about 18.6 mph), and
outside the towns 50 kmph (31 mph). Speed cameras
and alcohol breathalyzers have been introduced,
and may be used anywhere. On-the-spot-fines are
collected by uniformed police officers, who will
issue an official Malawi government receipt.

Breakdowns are indicated with signage, or with
a branch of a leafy tree—though this could also
be an indication of a funeral in a nearby village,
requiring one to slow down.

WHERE TO STAY

The country's largest hotel chain is Sunbird Hotels,
which has hotels at Majete Wildlife Reserve,
Blantyre, Zomba, Lilongwe, Mangochi, Salima,
and Mzuzu. The hotels are graded by the Tourism
Board from one to five stars. The largest hotel is the

President Walmont Hotel in Lilongwe. The other major hotels include Crossroads and Sagocea in Lilongwe, Ryalls and Victoria in Blantyre, and Grand Palace in Mzuzu.

There is cheaper, good-quality accommodation in most suburbs in the cities and major towns. Backpackers' lodges can be found mainly in Lilongwe and Blantyre and in some parts of the lakeshore area, and there are camping facilities along most of the beaches and in the game park areas.

Most rooms have mosquito nets, which should be used every night.

Most room prices include breakfast.

HEALTH

In Malawi free health care is available in all public hospitals, though their ability to cope with the demand is often challenged. For common health problems and fast diagnosis the public hospitals rely on Health Surveillance Assistants, who live in the communities, and who can quickly identify any breaking infections in their weekly reports. There are four tiers of public hospital. The highest is the central hospitals, with international standards of medicine. These are Kamuzu Central in the Central Region, Mzuzu Central in the north, and Zomba General and Queen Elizabeth Central in the south. Officially they are called referral hospitals. There are district hospitals in every district, save for Likoma and Blantyre, and then there are rural hospitals in the major trading centers. The last tier is made up of health centers in almost every other town or traditional authority.

The second-biggest health service provider is the Christian Health Association of Malawi (Cham), which runs a heavily subsidized, semi-public health service. They have a contract with the government to provide essential services where there is no public health provider. The main medical insurance provider is the Medical Aid Society of Malawi (MASM).

For a visitor in an emergency, there is an evacuation service to South Africa. Immunization against polio, tetanus, typhoid, and hepatitis A is advisable. If you came through a country where there is yellow fever, you may be required to show a certificate of immunization. The following few health issues require closer attention.

Malaria

Malaria is the common challenge, though anti-
malarial drugs can easily be bought in any pharmacy,
and using insect repellent and sleeping under
a mosquito net is the best form of protection.
Medication and quick diagnosis systems are readily
available across the country.

HIV/AIDS

HIV remains a public health concern, though
the number of infections has been going down.
Diagnostic services, including counseling and
treatment, are free in Malawi. The safest way to
avoid HIV infection is to be sure to use a condom
when engaging in sex.

Bilharzia

Bilharzia exists only where there is stagnant water
with a lot of water plants. Staying clear of stagnant

water beaches is the way to avoid it, though it is not as common as is often assumed. The risk is negligible near the main beach hotels. The infection is easily treated when diagnosed.

SAFETY AND SECURITY

Malawi is generally a very safe country for tourists and business travelers. Malawians are known for their friendly and warm-hearted nature. However, taking the usual precautions with valuables is always sensible, especially in the urban areas. It is strongly advised not to carry more valuables than necessary, to avoid attracting criminals. In terms of accommodation, it is best always to stay at a licensed lodging place.

Traveling at Night

Though it is generally safe to travel between cities, or from one point to another, short distances in dark and isolated areas should not be attempted. Ask for a taxi at the hotel reception desk, or plan to travel by day. For those going to clubs, having local friends or a guide to accompany you is advisable.

Always make sure your taxi is known to the lodge or your club bouncers for additional security. Again, don't carry any more money or valuables than you have to. Keep your bar cash separate from your taxi money, and show only the fare you have agreed to pay.

Dealing With the Police

The police can stop and search, and demand
any form of identity. There are, or may be,
uniformed police officers manning temporary
or permanent official roadblocks, some of which
are at the entrances to the major cities. The check
is straighforward and usually takes less than five
minutes. Some rogue officers might beg something
for "a drink," and it is up to the traveler to decide
how to react—whether to report the matter or to
ignore the request. There are no consequences for
foreigners if one simply answers that one is not
carrying any cash. The police have signed Malawi's
Public Service Charter and have reformed several
branches of their service, including the city 997
emergency line, victim support units, community
policing, and friendly services at the station, which
can all be helpful, depending on the nature of the
emergency.

EMERGENCY TELEPHONE NUMBERS
Police (city response) 997
Police (national response) 990
Ambulance 998
Fire department 999

chapter eight

BUSINESS BRIEFING

THE BUSINESS CLIMATE

Malawi has undertaken reforms, characterized by well-crafted policies and strategies, that have seen the country rise, year on year, to number 133 on the World Bank's Ease of Doing Business Index. Its biggest asset is its combination of political stability, investment security, legal framework, and a strong, independent judiciary.

The challenge has been the economy, which has been affected by the withdrawal of more than 40 percent of the donor budget after a financial scandal in 2013, and a series of natural disasters—including floods in 2015, drought in 2016—that hit its agricultural sector hard. Earnings from exports have suffered after poor sales of Malawi's number one export crop: tobacco. Inflation has been high—though is now falling—and the provision

of utilities such as electricity and water supplies remains a challenge. High bank rates have sent up the cost of borrowing.

The reforms, however, in terms of registration, competition, the tax regime, improved public finance management, economic diversification, and the liberalized economy, have attracted many manufacturing, agro-processing, and tourism investments. The mining industry has great potential, with an abundance of metals, gas, and oil that could improve the economy. Land can be leased or bought, depending on the nature of the investment.

Foreign partnership with local business is encouraged, as the locals have knowledge and expertise in the home market. Such businesses should be checked, and due diligence carried out on their financial records. Most local partners are honest in partnerships.

CHINESE AND INDIAN BUSINESSES
Chinese investment has grown since the political switch in diplomatic relations from Taiwan to Beijing in 2008, and has dominated the construction and retail sectors. The Chinese are now venturing into the processing of agricultural products, such as cotton and, partially, tobacco.

Indian businesses have links with Malawians of Indian origin, who have a long tradition of owning most of the shops in the major cities, trading in everything. Most Indian property owners have now abandoned retail shops and moved into real estate, hotels, transportation, and farming supplies.

Together, the two groups control the manufacturing sectors, agro-supplies, construction, hotels, and to a certain extent government contracts, as most of the funding is by concessional lines of credit from their respective governments, restricting tenders to such companies.

DEALING WITH GOVERNMENT AND PUBLIC AGENCIES

The government has been undertaking public service reforms to address long-standing complaints of delays, bureaucracy, and poor follow-up and responses to issues. Most public service agencies have different layers of officials. Depending on the nature of the issue, the best approach is to deal with the appropriate local authority. If the matter is agricultural, rushing to the minster or the principal secretary might yield some movement, but it is the officers on the ground who will deliver results. Today, with decentralization, they have the budgets and powers to make decisions affecting their jurisdiction. In the case of high-level projects, middlemen who claim to have access to State House or public officials should always be viewed with suspicion, and the best option is to approach the formal agencies directly.

INVESTMENT PROCEDURE

Malawi has established a one-stop-shop business start-up and investment center, where all investment procedures can be processed. The Malawi Investment and Trade Centre (MITC) coordinates the issue of business permits (by an immigration specialist within the One Stop Service Centre), the processing of business residence permits, and temporary employment permits, applications, and approvals. It further coordinates the sourcing of joint-venture partners, domestic and foreign, for both Malawian and international companies, provides general business advice, and manages business incentives available to investors. The MITC organizes an annual Malawi Investment Forum in October and publishes a compendium of readily available projects for prospective investors.

THE BUSINESS CULTURE

The largest locally owned firm is the Press Corporation, which at one point controlled 30 percent of the economy and had a footprint in banking, agriculture, property, retail, beverages, pharmaceuticals, and food processing. The liberalization of the economy has introduced a competitive business culture, with family businesses (mainly owned by Asians) adopting proper structures and diversifying into various sectors of the economy.

The Malawi Confederation of Chambers of Commerce and Industry is a major private sector organization for institutions with a strong corporate culture and an attractive platform for most business start-ups as it provides various services to its membership. Sector groups, such as the Farmers' Union of Malawi, the Tea Association of Malawi, the Tobacco Association of Malawi, the Indigenous Business Owners' Association, and the Transporters' Association of Malawi, use different approaches— some corporate and others protectionist. Owing to the relatively small size of the manufacturing sector, most industries are interlinked, and business portfolios usually include a diversity of fields.

BUSINESS DRESS
Formal wear—suit and tie, and the equivalent for women—is in all cases appropriate for business meetings, apart from those involving field or agricultural visits. On Fridays, most business staff adopt printed shirts or traditional wear.

SETTING UP APPOINTMENTS
Personal relations are all-important. If you want to meet a certain individual for business, it is very helpful to meet socially first. It is quite acceptable to make a direct approach at a social event, such as a party, and then follow up. Otherwise, for an initial business contact it is better to visit the office personally and find someone to talk to rather than sending an e-mail or making a telephone call. For foreigners who have never been to the country, contacting the

Malawi Embassy, the MITC, or a sector-specific agency is important, as they can introduce you to the appropriate individuals or offices.

After making appointments with senior public officials you will need to confirm the dates and times occasionally because their calendars tend to be fluid, meaning their arrangements might change at any time.

MEETINGS

It is important to arrive early for a meeting, as this will allow you to chat with the "other side." If the meeting involves a higher authority, you will go through some kind of briefing or pre-assessment of your presentation. At the meeting the visitor will always sit opposite the head of the delegation. Your presentation should highlight the basic issues, the solution, and the figures. Your projections should be realistic. If your proposal includes getting a necessary permit

and/or processes such as an environmental impact assessment, you should outline these requirements and give an assessment of how long they are likely to take to acquire. Politicians want quick results, so bear in mind that your project could be announced to the public even before the financing has been sourced. It is important to be clear as to whether yours is just a proposal, or whether financing is already in place. Most projects with ready financing or minimal processes will have the quick endorsement of public officials. Avoid suggesting one-to-one meetings at the start; these may be misconstrued, and should be offered by the hosts.

NEGOTIATIONS
Business negotiations will be prolonged if the key decision makers are not involved at the beginning. Try to find out who can move things forward. Use informal discussions to find out what their demands or positions are, so that you can start easily with the areas you all agree on. If the negotiations involve acquisitions or major contracts, having good references can speed up the process. The most important aspect of negotiating is to gain the confidence and trust of the other side.

CONTRACTS AND FULFILLMENT
Though Malawi has a mixture of common and civil law, its contract law is all primarily based on written legislation. It has a strong and independent

legal system that guarantees contract enforcement and fulfillment. For contractors tendering for government business, funding could be a challenge—it is necessary to consider risks such as currency fluctuations or delayed funding and to make allowances for them in the contract in order to minimize losses. The High Court has a commercial division to speed up the resolution of business disputes, and the Industrial Relations Court is a labor court designed to ensure minimal delays caused by workplace issues. Malawi is a signatory to various international instruments guaranteeing the validity of contracts and enforcement at both domestic and international levels.

WOMEN IN BUSINESS

Despite the fact that women have been prominent in most powerful public institutions—starting with President Joyce Banda, a Chief Justice (retired), an Attorney General, and Clerks of Parliament— the roles of women in business have largely been confined to small-scale entrepreneurship, rather than being part of an overall shift in corporate culture.

Notable female chief executives have been appointed at Toyota Malawi, Nation Publications, and NBS Bank. There are company secretaries and marketing managers, but the top management positions remain male-dominated, despite efforts at gender equality. The biggest obstacle has been the absence of women managers outside working hours, as most business negotiations are undertaken in informal settings. The trend is different in Malawi's diplomatic and international organizations, many of which have been headed by women who have managed to do business with male-dominated structures across the country.

GIFT GIVING

Gifts are acceptable in a business transaction if they are not outrageously valuable. Simple bottles of wine, day planners, crafts or products from your country, or company-inscribed items would not raise eyebrows. Branded corporate gifts are welcome at the first meeting, as many businesses would have a Malawian gift ready for the guests.

CORRUPTION

Corruption has become a major governance issue in Malawi. Most cases concern pure theft and fraud. The biggest scandals were in procurement and the awarding of contracts, until 2011, when a fraud ring was caught siphoning public funds in a collusion between accounts personnel and some private companies. In September 2013, the shooting of a budget director in the treasury uncovered a US $30 million scandal (dubbed "Cashgate") in which more than one hundred individuals, public officers, politicians, businesses and others colluded to loot public coffers to finance the then ruling party's campaign. Most of the suspects were arrested, tried, and jailed. Some of the suspects are still awaiting trial. The scandal has brought closer public scrutiny of public contracts, and bribe-seeking behavior is now very unlikely in the awarding of major contracts.

The Anti-Corruption Bureau's focus is now on education and awareness to prevent service bribes— such as bribing traffic police when you are stopped, or to allow you to cut in line at a road traffic tailback, or offering a bribe to speed up passport applications, to get preferential consideration applying for land or housing, and even, in the case of tobacco farmers, to be given priority when selling their produce at auction. The bribery syndicates were limited to specific departments, and with intense media exposure they have been radically reduced. Though the country is not fully corruption free, the investigations, arrests, and jailing of suspects indicate that Malawi's anti-corruption efforts are bearing fruit, as compared to many other African countries.

Foreign businesspeople may at times find themselves competing with Indian or Chinese companies who allegedly offer huge bribes to be awarded contracts. If asked for a bribe, they should report it to the Anti-Corruption Bureau, and it will be taken seriously.

chapter nine

COMMUNICATING

LANGUAGE

English is the official language of Malawi, and people generally speak and understand it, even in the rural areas. Literacy rates have improved in recent years, and now stands at 65 percent. This has resulted in English being even more widespread.

Chichewa is the national language, and is the only vernacular widely spoken and taught in schools. There are many other languages and dialects, the most widely spoken being Lhomwe, Sena, Yao, Senga, Tumbuka, Ngonde, Tonga, and Ndali. Chitipa, the most northerly district, has more than nine languages. If you greet people in the local language this always impresses them and will quickly endear you to them.

As we have seen, the Malawian pronunciation of English words can have surprising results. For example, for Malawians the name of the Shire (River) becomes "Shiii…lee."

FORMS OF ADDRESS AND GREETINGS

Addressing people by their formal title is *de rigueur*. At official functions those in charge of protocol will have the correct form of address for everyone present. When you greet people who have a title, such as Honorable, Right Honorable, Doctor, or Professor, you should be sure to get it right. Never address a chief as "Mr."—find out the appropriate form of address for any chief you might be meeting. In conversations, do not ever ask what field their doctorate or professorship is in. Some of them could be honorary or even bogus titles, and they might feel you are trying to embarrass them.

As we have seen, greetings in Malawi can be a formal and extended process. They depend on the status of your counterpart. If you meet someone older than yourself, or senior to you, you are expected to greet them politely, formally, and correctly. This starts with the process of identification, when they ask who you are. You are expected to answer all questions politely, and offer a little more information. By tradition, you should inquire about the welfare of their family or homestead that day. If you meet on a road (especially walking) the greetings might include questions about your reason for heading in that direction—for example, whether it is just a visit or whether someone is sick. For official greetings, using correct titles and making a little bow when offered a handshake will help.

BODY LANGUAGE
Body language is very important. Standing stiffly in the presence of a senior is considered to show respect, and a formal attitude should be maintained

HUMOR

There is a lot of poking fun at people from other regions in Malawi. The north of the country, which is more innovative and quick to adopt foreign names, is often the butt of jokes. Northerners who have traveled abroad often give their children foreign place names, such as Southwood, Scotland, or Texas. So now, whenever something particular, such as elections or new technology, is in the news, other Malawians will say that babies born in the north will probably be called "Rigging" or "4G Munthali."

What Did You Learn?

Children, especially boys, learn at an early age how men spend their time, and the following story comes from a teacher working in a Ngoni school. Teacher to students: "One bucket of water and one bucket of liquor are placed in front of a donkey. The donkey drinks the water and leaves the liquor. What does this teach us?"

Little Mboba puts both hands up and answers as follows: "One who does not drink liquor is a donkey."

The Preacher and the Guard

The coming in of Pentecostal Churches has livened up services, many of which are long, and often conducted in rented premises. Most preachers claim to speak to and bring special messages from God in services that include deliverance—where evil spirits are cast out—special prayers, and prophecies.

A certain fire-and-brimstone preacher, whose services lasted hours, used to fill the City Hall with his followers. One Sunday, he decided to prolong the service, and people started drifting away. By 4:00 p.m., only the choir and a few elders remained. An hour later, only his wife and one old man were left. He continued, in full flood. His wife left. At 6:00 p.m., seeing only the man at the back of the hall, he loudly proclaimed, "I saw you as a man of faith in my vision. God has told me to deliver a special blessing to one who will endure and remain. He has asked me to ordain you as a high priest, with more blessings to follow." He approached the old man and said, "Are you ready for your anointing?"

The old man, taken aback, replied, "I am sorry, Man of God, I am simply a city guard, waiting for you to finish so that I can lock up the hall."

Between Church and Work

One Wednesday afternoon the boss walked into Mr. Phiri's office and asked him if he could come to work on Saturday and Sunday. Mr. Phiri was a very staunch Adventist who never missed church on Saturdays. However, since he could not say no to his boss, he replied, "No problem, I will probably be late, though, as public transportation is really bad on weekends where I live." The boss answered, "That is okay, but what time do you think you will get here?" Mr. Phiri replied, "By Monday morning, Sir."

throughout the encounter. A more relaxed stance can be misinterpreted as meaning you don't acknowledge their presence. When introducing yourself, don't come too close to anybody—give them personal space. Tactile behavior, such as patting someone on the back, should be restricted to people you already know. Flamboyant gestures, such as talking with one's hands, or pointing at people, are not considered appropriate.

THE MEDIA

Malawi has a vibrant and free media. The biggest challenges have been media ownership and the low incomes of journalists, which have often affected the integrity and professionalism of the output.

The Press

Malawi has two major newspapers, both privately owned—*Nation* and *The Daily Times*. These two companies continue to monopolize the print media, with occasional, usually partisan, tabloids coming and going. The two papers have crossed paths with different administrations, as they are both owned by political families, both Bandas. Nation Publications Limited is owned by the family of the late Aleke Banda, a rare principled politician, who ironically, prior to independence in 1959, founded *Malawi News*, which is part of the Times Group, owned by the family of the late Hastings Kamuzu Banda.

The press in Malawi is free, but there has been occasional friction with the political establishment, that has seen both papers, at different times, being subjected to advertising bans and their journalists arrested, threatened, or beaten. The strong and vocal Malawi chapter of the media advocacy organization Media Institute of Southern Africa has ensured that a free press is sustained. Legislation to guarantee access to Information took fifteen years to pass in Parliament, with successive governments creating delays or trying to water it down. It was enacted in 2017.

There are several colonial-era provisions of the penal code that have been identified as impeding the freedom of the press, but there has been very little appetite among politicians for the removal of the statutes.

Broadcast Media

There are more than fifteen licensed television stations, most of them religious. Only five have national coverage, but this has no meaningful impact as the number of TV sets has remained below 1.5 million in a population of 18 million. Limited access to electricity and competition from satellite TV means that most of the stations target a selected audience. TV is mainly watched for soccer and soaps, other than being a source of news. Local content remains limited, as most of the private TV companies struggle with operating costs.

There are eighty licensed radio stations, many of which are dedicated to religious and community outreach. Radio is the major source of news for the majority, and coverage for the state-owned Malawi Broadcasting Corporation (MBC), which has TV and two radio channels, is around 95 percent. The privately owned Zodiak Broadcasting Corporation has TV, radio, and online presence. Zodiak has become authoritative, especially in broadcasting election results. Other influential broadcast media includes the commercially oriented Capital Radio, Malawi Institute of Journalism (MIJ) radio, and the all-music channel Power 101FM. The broadcasters rely heavily on local content, as their focus is limited to their audience. All major faiths have launched their own radio stations.

The major challenge has been political control of the taxpayer-funded MBC as successive governments have refused to open it up to opposition views. Sometimes national television and radio broadcast outrageous political propaganda. In protest opposition parties in parliament have allocated a symbolic one kwacha for its annual budget. The broadcast media has peculiar ownership, with all Malawi's presidents (dead or alive) owning a broadcast platform. This at times has led to all-out unethical broadcasts, threats, and blatant propaganda. The Kamuzu family owns 100 percent of the Times broadcast platforms Times TV and Times Radio; the second President Bakili Muluzi's family owns and runs the Joy Media Group, comprised of TV and radio; the Mutharika family (the third and fifth presidents) own the Galaxy Broadcasting Corporation, with a TV license and a live radio, and the fourth president Joyce Banda's family is linked to Ufulu Radio and holds a TV license as well. The independent radios, however, have opened up the airwaves to phone-in programs, tough interviews, and challenging points of view, which has led at times to the Malawi Communications Regulatory Authority being accused of being used to intimidate those seen to be broadcasting anti-ruling party views. The other agency used to intimidate the media is the tax collection body, the Malawi Revenue Authority.

Online News

All the major media houses have an online and social media presence. You can listen to live broadcasts for most stations including MBC, Zodiak, Capital, Radio Maria Malawi, Radio Islam, and Times Radio. These are credible sources of information about Malawi. The BBC's Focus on Africa and other major international media outlets carry periodic updates on major news and current affairs in Malawi. However, there has been an infiltration of online news outlets with some mixing of factual stories with political or personal propaganda. It is therefore important to verify most of the reports carried by online media with other media platforms. The Nation, Capital FM, and Zodiak have live social media updates, and most breaking news can be verified on their platforms. The common new sites include Nyasatimes, Malawi Voice, Maravi Post, and Malawi24. The sites have sometimes attracted attention with anonymously written political features. The Internet freedom has, however, brought with it "fake news," and the visitor should take sensational online news stories with a pinch of salt.

SERVICES

Mail and Courier Services

The Malawi Post Corporation (MPC) runs 180 post offices throughout the country, and provides mail and other services. Owing to the lack of street addresses, all mail is delivered to and collected from post office boxes.

International and city-to-city deliveries are also available through courier services such as DHL, FedEx, UPS, Post Office, Axa, Times, and others across the country. Door-to-door services are available for most courier companies.

Internet

The Internet is still expensive in Malawi, although cell phone coverage has increased, including 4G network. Wi-Fi is available at all major hotels and some government buildings; however, in the rural areas access is better with cell phones or dongles (portable modems) provided by the cell phone companies. Fiber optic has been extended across the country to reduce Internet costs.

Malawians are very quick to adopt new technology, and the latest technology is readily available. The growing presence and use of social media have affected the efficiency of public services delivery and official announcements, such as road closures, or services cuts, and been a spur to social activism. Most of the key social media platforms are a vital source of information.

Telephone

There are two landline (fixed) telephone providers: Malawi Telecommunications Ltd, and Access

Communications. Between them they cover only 1.9 percent of the population. The companies offer Internet connections with good speeds and are cheaper than most other providers.

There are two cell phone companies in Malawi: Airtel and TNM. These companies have progressed well, with at least 3 million subscribers between them. Most people are thought to have two lines split between the two companies. The cell phone solutions include increased Internet access and availability,  and online banking, which has improved access to finances, particularly for those operating in rural areas. The cost of calls has now been offset by Internet alternatives such as WhatsApp and Skype. The best option is to buy data bundles, which are cheaper than pay-as-you-go. SIM cards can be bought anywhere, even on the streets.

CONCLUSION

The most friendly, welcoming, and smiling people, Malawians provide the best example of the African concept of *umunthu* (community sharing). They have a rare spirit. One of the most diverse nations in terms of tribal makeup, they have come together to create a society of peace and tranquility, open both to foreigners seeking fun and to those seeking shelter. Malawi is never mentioned in the same breath as other well-known African holiday destinations, but almost everyone who has had a chance to visit it has fallen in love with it and returned—many even to settle, work, or volunteer. The country has everything one could wish for in an African experience—the unspoiled nature, a celebrated culture, and a fascinating history, each region offering its own range of attractions.

Malawi is among the least-developed countries, and many of its people live in deep poverty. The smiling and joking of mothers with babies strapped on their backs, however, show the perseverance and good humor of a people who have experienced dictatorship and have at times been let down by their political leaders and even by foreign donors.

As more and more Malawians gain access to information, from basic life skills to new technologies, many become wary of the "interventionist attitudes" of outsiders. They welcome changes that improve their lives. They frown at ideas that they find culturally, sometimes religiously, unacceptable. Positive, honest, hardworking, and community minded, they will embrace change at their own rate.

Further Reading

Benson, C. W. and P. M. Benson. *The Birds of Malawi*. Limbe, Malawi: Montfort Press, 1977.

Boucher Chisale, C. *The Gospel Seed: Culture and Faith in Malawi as Expressed in the Missio Banner*. Mua Mission, Malawi: KuNgoni Art Craft Centre, 2002.

—— *Digging our Roots. The Chamare Museum Frescoes*. Mua Mission, Malawi: KuNgoni Art Craft Centre, 2002.

—— *When Animals Sing and Spirits Dance. Gule Wamkulu. The Great Dance of the Chewa People of Malawi*. Oxford: Kungoni Centre of Culture and Art, 2012.

Buckler, M. L. *From Microsoft to Malawi: Learning on the Front Lines as a Peace Corps Volunteer*. Lanham, MD, USA: Hamilton Books, 2011.

Johnson, Sigrid A. *Nyika; A Guide to Nyika National Park, Malawi*. Biddenden, Kent, England: Nyika-Vwaza Trust, 2017.

Kamkwamba, W. and B. Mealer. *The Boy who Harnessed the Wind*. London, UK: HarperCollins, 2010.

Konings, Ad. *Malawi Cichlids in their Natural Habitat*, 4th Edition. Malawi, Cichlid Press, 2007.

McCracken, John. *A History of Malawi, 1859-1966*. Sufolk, England: James Curry, 2010.

Mapanje, Jack. *Of Chameleons and Gods*. London, UK: Heinemann's African Writers Series, 1981.

Ross, Andrew. *Colonialism to Cabinet Crisis; A Political History of Malawi*. Zomba, Malawi: Kachere, 2009.

Ross, Kenneth R. *Christianity in Malawi, A Source Book*. Mambo, Zimbabwe: Kachere, 1996.

Smithers, R. H. N. *The Mammals of Rhodesia, Zambia and Malawi*. London, UK: Collins, 1966.

culture smart! malawi

Index

Acknowledgments

To Barry Tomalin, my teacher and mentor in International Communications, Kelly White of Malawi Tourism for the passion in presenting Malawi as the eighth wonder of the world, and Ian Musyani and his many stories about the people in the North. Senior Chief Lukwa, the Right Honourable Dr. Justin Malewezi, and the Chewa Heritage Foundation for keeping the Chewa culture alive. To Kondwani Kamiyala, Emmanuel Kondwerani Luciano, Remmie Ng'omba, and Tim Duncane Zambezi for their support.